# ENERGY MERGING

# ENERGY MERGING

A healing modality based in oneness.
Oneness: another word for Love.

by Marc Peridis
Inspired by the teachings of Kenneth Ray Stubbs

First edition, 2024
Published by Marc Peridis LTD.
Copyright © 2024 Marc Peridis Ltd
19 Greek Street, London,
W1D 4DT
www.orgasmicshaman.com



ISBN: 978-1-0369-0469-2
Imprint: Independently published

# ACKNOWLEDGEMENTS

I dedicate this book to Kenneth Ray Stubbs for being an inspiration, for being the first to teach me the process of energy merging and for being a trailblazer in this field. Dear Sex Shaman, Sacred Prostitute, you are missed.

I also dedicate this book to all the other students of Kenneth Ray Stubbs, more specifically, the more committed students of the Rainbow Body Circle, who walk the world as living and breathing legacy-holders of this important work.

I also dedicate this book to the many students who have shown up since I began teaching in 2016 to learn this practice before I could even express it in words.

I also thank my teacher Cass Phelps, who, since 2015, has provided a container to explore energy merging within somatic practice beyond the shamanic realm. Thank you for being an example of teaching by transmission.

I thank my friend and peer, Reverend Goddess Charmaine, for the endless moments we spent sitting and merging energetically, holding each other in light as we walked our paths side by side.

Finally, thank you to all the clients, followers and supporters of my work, who may have just viewed a quick online video or committed to years of professional training. Your encouragement means the world to me.

# CONTENTS

# INTRODUCTION

When the shaman paused and looked up from her drum, I was struck by the words she spoke next:

"You are a shaman," she said confidently.
"You are one of us."

It was June 2015 and I had recently left my life as a London interior designer to pursue a journey towards an unknown purpose. While I had a strong sense that I was being led to a more altruistic and less superficial life, "shaman" didn't figure on the list of potential career options.

I moved to Barcelona. Within weeks of arriving, Honi, an American shaman with whom I had previously worked, came to visit. She said she had a strong sense that we needed to spend time together but neither of us understood why. It became clear one morning at the end of a sunrise ceremony on the beach.

"You are a shaman, you are one of us."

"So what do I do now?" I asked.

"Nothing. Just wait."

These instructions felt excruciating for someone used to fast-paced London where things either happened or they didn't. But indeed, all I had to do was wait.

Within 24 hours, a peculiar series of circumstances (I will share later in this book) unfolded, and the path was drawn before me.

It all culminated a few months later in Brazil when fate decided to fling me into a shamanic mission with Marie and Sylvain, two other (much more experienced) shamans I didn't know. Our time together was wild, filled with moments that were at times ecstatic, at times scary, and at other times completely surreal. To this day, I still don't fully understand exactly what we did or what our purpose was, but I remember how significant it felt.

Led mainly by Marie, the most experienced of the three of us, we would sit and listen for our inner guidance, informing us about the details of our journey. It would guide us on where to go and what to do and even provide us with a precise schedule.

We would climb to the top of a mountain in the blazing afternoon sun to bury a sacred stone.

We would chant and drum in a freezing waterfall at sundown.

We would meditate on a 2-billion-year-old rock formation at 3:33 pm, informed and bewildered by the hallucinations that would arise.

With time, our purpose became clearer.

As we communed with the land, we were enabling a connection to another realm some might call the divine, Source, or quantum. We were helping to create a bridge, an access point on earth, for those who might feel called to connect to it.

We connected to the wisdom of ancient civilisations like the ancient Egyptians and ancient Greeks, who believed, like us, that certain specific spots on earth were more powerful than others. These were known as power spots. Sacred sites, such as the famous temples of Greece, the pyramids of Egypt, and structures such as Stonehenge were apparently built to intensify the energy that was already present at these sites. Visiting these gives us access to a greater power.

**Enter the sexual shaman.**

On one of our last nights, a surprisingly pivotal moment came when my colleagues spoke in unison that they felt intuitively I was a "sex shaman". I still didn't fully know what a shaman was, but for the last 5 years I had been on a path of learning tantra and sexual healing, so, it made sense somehow.

Off the back of this conversation, Sylvain suggested I get in touch with Kenneth Ray Stubbs, an Arizona-based man in his mid-seventies who many referred to as the "Sexual Shaman."

Ray was a force of nature.

As an Academic, he was a doctor of Sociology and Sexology.

Originally from Alabama, a hippy trip led him to work in a porn theatre and eventually to learn massage therapy in Mexico. His teachers taught him to avoid the genital area, which he felt left an important part of the body ignored. He began to wonder what could happen if sexual energy was allowed rather than suppressed. Better yet, what if it could be heightened and flood across the entire body rather than considered non-existent?

This inquiry led him to become one of the few pioneers in the San Francisco Bay Area to experiment with integrating the genitals into the full-body massage in the early 1970s. According to Stubbs, he was the first to coin the term erotic massage and went on to write and publish various books and documentaries, including one he claims was the first to feature photography of genital massage.

However, what impressed me the most about Ray was not the books he had written, the documentaries he filmed, or the fact that he had been a pioneer in a field I deeply respected. It was the power of his mere presence.

**I'll never forget the first time we "met."**

I called the Skype number I found on his website, assuming it would lead to a voice box asking me to leave a message or send an email. To my surprise, he picked up right away.

We didn't have the time to speak but scheduled a longer call the following day.

Upon hanging up from that short call I was blown away. I sat paralysed in front of my screen, and my mind dissolved. My entire body was flooded by a stream of electric sensations which ran up and down in waves and tingled beneath the layers of my skin. It felt ecstatic and blissful as if I was being transported to another realm.

I had felt this before, but never in such a casual context. I experienced it in Brazil during a ceremony or while meditating at sacred sites. But I never experienced such strong and blissful energy simply by being in someone's virtual presence for less than 30 seconds.

In Brazil, my colleagues and I discussed ancient civilisations that lived according to the principle that humans could support the healing and transformation of others simply by their focused intention and presence.

This concept deeply resonated with me. It felt right to me that, like other beings in nature, a flower, a fruit, or even the venom of a snake, we humans, too, should be able to yield impact effortlessly, simply with the power of our presence and nothing else.

But this was contrary to the societal structures which had taught me that anything worthwhile could only result from experiencing challenge and sacrifice, that only a race for success would guarantee my survival, and that the journey should inevitably be effortful and painful.

This philosophy, in contrast, felt radical, refreshing and promising.

While Stubbs knew little about these civilisations and their philosophies, he was, without a doubt, the first person I met who embodied this idea. So much so, in fact, that a mere 30-second video call left me feeling something I could only describe as pure oneness.

I spoke about this with Ray the following day. He chuckled and looked away from the screen.

"That is my work." He said. "That is energy."

In 1991, an accident left him paralysed, unable to move his legs or arms. No longer able to teach his body-based work, he turned to Buddhism and shamanism and was led to develop a practice that was fully based on energetic development.

By the time I met Ray, I had completed a one-year tantra training and many years of training in the somatic movement practice of Continuum Movement, rooted in the connection to Source.

Hearing I might be a sex shaman led me to consider other training courses such as sexological bodywork, body electric, and the Taoist training by Mantak Chia.

Conceptually, these trainings all made sense. Each offered a framework of tools and skills I could apply to future clients to support healing and impact. But what Ray offered was literally beyond words: it was simply transmission.

Ray became one of my main teachers, and most of the teaching over the years happened via transmission, simply by sitting together and sharing energy.

It was a practice of energy merging.

Over these years, I developed a practice of sacred intimacy and sacred sexuality, which involves somatic therapy, shamanism and sexual explorations. Energy merging is at the root of it.

In November 2023, Kenneth Ray Stubbs passed away, leaving behind a rich legacy, including a collection of books, crystals and, most importantly, the impact thousands had felt from his work.

Many of the great names in sexual healing carry a piece of his legacy today, which is still passed on to thousands of students and participants in workshops around the world.

When he died, I felt called to step up. I felt inspired to birth something new without knowing exactly what it would be.

Stubbs was clear; he never wanted anyone to teach his work his way and would not pass down his practices for anyone to teach verbatim. Not because he didn't believe anyone would be capable, but simply because he felt strongly that each of us is meant to bring our gifts and teachings in our own unique way.

A few months after his death, the invitation to birth something new began to intensify. I heard an inner voice that sounded masculine and soft speaking to me. Perhaps it was Ray's, maybe mine, or someone else's.

"Don't you see what are you really here to bring?" The voice spoke. "Don't you see?"

These words confused me until clarity came while teaching a workshop in Spain in June 2024. The participants and I entered a deep non-verbal meditation process called a "deep dive" that lasted 24 hours.

While I did my best to push aside anything distracting me from holding space for the group, a clear and strong vision came. It was a small rectangular paperback book, thin, less than two hundred pages, with the words "Energy Merging" on the cover. The vision was so clear that it felt as if it was already published.

I had no choice; it was going to be written.

I realised that the voice asking me to "remember what I was here to bring" was inviting me to share an aspect of my work that was central to it but that I seldom spoke of:

Energy Merging.

Energy merging was the practice that took place as I sat with Ray for years and years. It also happened at sacred sites and temples and on the missions with the other shamans in Brazil.

It is a shamanic practice and a healing modality by which we intend to be one:

One with parts of ourselves,
One with others,
One with all of existence.

It is a practice based in the unseen, non-local part of our universe we can't feel or touch, but we know it exists: the essence of all existence.

According to my knowledge, this practice has never been formalised by Stubbs or any of his students, and this is not the aim of this book. I believe energy merging is too central to our human nature for anyone to attempt to capture or own it.

Instead, this book intends to share this practice openly, to allow it to be seen and known, to exist alongside the many other energy practices that benefit so many around the world.

Despite training in many modalities and experiencing various others, no other practice has impacted me more than energy merging.

When I have felt lost, when everything has seemed broken or fallen apart, it has always led me back home, back to oneness and back to love.

The idea that oneness would be healing makes sense. Anything that needs healing or transformation has inevitably disconnected from oneness or wholeness somehow. In fact, the words whole and heal share the same linguistic origins. The root of the word whole is "hāl" in old English, which is also the root of the word heal. Healing is a process of restoring wholeness.

This book includes theories inspired by Ray's teachings and others arising from other research and experimentation. It is written from my perspective and was written after his death, so he didn't contribute to, approve, or even read it.

I am undoubtedly expressing and sharing a vision different from his. My version of energy merging is infused with knowledge from the worlds of somatic therapy and sexual healing which has melted into it over the years.

I hope it will inspire and serve you. I also wish any student of the practice to feel free to experience, share and teach it their way.

Some parts of the book will be more technical and scientific, and perhaps even confusing. I invite you to keep at it. At the end, it's always about love.

Chapter 1 begins with the basics: What is energy? How is it experienced? How has scientific theory explained it? If we, and everything around us, are energy, how do we experience our energetic being? We will also explore the composition of our universe, the local, the non-local and the 5 planes of existence.

Chapter 2 introduces oneness. What is oneness? How do we experience it as humans? How does it benefit us? It speaks of the science of merging, transmission and intending to be one.

Chapter 3 introduces the energy being. An energy being has experienced sufficient energetic development, allowing them to share their abilities with others. We will also explore various archetypal interpretations of the energy being, such as the shaman, the sacred prostitute and even Jesus Christ.

Chapter 4 explores our energy body. In addition to having physical bodies, each of us has an energy body composed of various energetic structures. Developing and awakening these structures allows us to become an energy being.

Chapter 5 introduces the process of energy merging. We will then explore the 3 main types of energy merging practice:

- Merging with Source and all of existence
- Merging with parts of ourselves
- Merging with others as an act of space-holding

Chapter 6 focuses on the first type, merging with Source. It teaches us that the intentional act of being one with all of existence can allow us to develop our energetic abilities and to be one with more energy. We develop, grow, and gain more resources. We are able "to be one with" more of life.

Chapter 7 focuses on the second type, merging with ourselves. It shares the importance of intending to be one with every part of the self. Using the resources we develop from merging with Source, we can intend to be one with anything within us that needs attention; any challenge, issue, distortion or pain. We will explore the relationship between energy merging, healing and trauma.

Chapter 8 focuses on the third type, merging with others. Once we have developed enough energetic capability, we can intend to be one with others and hold space for them, supporting their healing and transformation.

Chapter 9 shares my story of becoming an energy being as a case study, from first experiencing oneness in 2010 to an initiation to shamanism, the years of mentoring with Kenneth Ray Stubbs, and developing my practice as a sex shaman, sacred prostitute.

This book is for those who want to engage with Source more deeply and explore how this connection can support their and others' development as space-holders and facilitators. Most of all, it aims to show us we are more than we think. Each of us has the potential to connect with and benefit from the energy of all existence at every moment.

We can all be in the world, deeply engaging with circumstances, challenges, pleasure and pain while knowing we are also held and supported by a power greater than all of it.

We can access the ability to see the gift in everything; that no matter how challenging things might appear at first, everything is exactly as it should be.

In our truth, each one of us has the potential to be an energy being and yield a healing impact on others simply by the power of our very presence.

# 1

## WHAT IS ENERGY?

When I speak of energy, I do not refer to caloric intake or the energy needed to run up a flight of stairs, make love, or operate a chainsaw. I am referring to energy as the invisible life force behind all existence.

Energy refers to the world of the unseen, the part of existence beyond the form that we can see, touch, and measure; that is beyond the understanding of the mind.

For instance, we often refer to feeling a certain vibe in the room. Statements like "you could cut the tension with a knife…" usually denote a dense and unpleasant energy. Or we might comment that we like someone's energy more than someone else's.

Sometimes, we notice that while two people might utter similar words and behave in ways that appear similar, one will feel attractive and magnetic to us, and the other will not. This difference is often based on energy.

But energy is much more than this pleasant or unpleasant feeling, it is the primordial way we connect to ourself, to each other and to all of existence.

Its understanding begins by acknowledging that existence is made of vibrating frequencies. What we see as solid is only a small part of reality. According to Carlo Rovelli, physicist and author of the bestseller The Order of Time, "The world is not made of stones, but rather light, energy, sounds, or waves moving through the sea."

In The Physics of God, author Joseph Selbie compiles studies and theories that demonstrate and support this.

**Quantum theory**

If you have been called to a book on energy, you may have previously heard that, according to quantum theory, our human bodies, the earth and everything surrounding us comprise 99.9999999% energy. If we were to remove the empty space or energy from our bodies, we would end up with a ball of matter the size of the head of a pin. If we were to remove it from the entire earth, we would end up with a ball the size of an orange.

**The theory of relativity**

In 1905, Albert Einstein published a paper explaining his theory of special relativity. In it, he wrote that the nucleus of an atom was actually a super-condensed, super-high-frequency form of energy. He was the first to prove that matter doesn't exist.

## The energy-verse, potentia and the spiritual world

Selbie also speaks of the energy-verse as the scientific version of the heavens of all religious traditions. It is where we live after death and where angelic beings dwell.

Nobel prize winner Werner Heisenberg, who famously authored the theory of uncertainty, spoke of potentia as the part of the energy-verse which interacts with our universe. It is the unseen realm behind all matter, from where all life springs and forms.

If the energy-verse and potentia ceased to exist, the universe would as well.

This was also demonstrated through the concept of correspondence by scientist Emanuel Swedenborg. The natural world and everything in it arise from and are sustained by the spiritual world. Both come from the divine.

## Local vs. non-local

These studies point to what Selbie describes as local vs. non-local realms. The local is bound by space or time. It relates to everything that can be seen, touched, and measured. For instance, the size and weight of a lemon, the speed at which it drops from the tree, and even the light thumping sound it makes as it drops to the earth all belong to the local.

The non-local is not bound by space or time. It is the part we can't see, measure or understand but know exists. It is the mysterious force that turns a seed into a small plant, then into a tree, that then grows lemons that drop from the tree. This belongs to the non-local. Non-locality is a fundamental property of the cosmos.

From non-local intelligent consciousness comes the information that creates the holographic, cosmic movie we know as the universe. Everything exists in both of these realms.

## The wave/particle duality

Author Carlo Rovelli's idea that all form, even the hardest stone, is made of frequencies vibrating relates to the wave/particle duality. It speaks of the fact that all waves can become particles, and all particles are originally waves.

In the 17th century, English Physicist Sir Isaac Newton first proposed that light is made of particles, a theory supported and demonstrated by various subsequent studies.

This was most famously demonstrated by the double-slit experiments, first conducted by Thomas Young in 1801. It studied the way particles such as photons and electrons behaved when projected through the slits cut out of a panel, landing onto a solid back panel. Scientists were surprised to find that the particles sometimes behaved like form, and other times they behaved like light waves.

In 1924, French physicist Louis de Broglie spoke of the wave/particle duality, which suggested that electrons and all matter could be considered waves.

Knowing that everything, even the hardest stone, originates as a wave leads us to an important truth: the world is not as solid as we perceive it to be. Transformation and change can, therefore, happen more easily than we think.

Think about the effort that would be required to change the shape of a stone. It would break to pieces if it were pressed with the right tools. Yet, by contrast, a ray of light, or the waves of the sea, move easily and gently under our breath and change shape as we move our hands.

**Intensity and consciousness**

The double-slit experiment, which demonstrated that all waves can become particles and that all particles are originally waves, also speaks of the intelligent observer.

The result, by which some particles behaved as particles, and others behaved as waves, varied depending on whether a sensor was present to track specific results. The sensor added an element of expectation of certain outcomes, which impacted the results.

This element became known as the intelligent observer, which relates to the idea that a researcher's expectation of results will impact the study's results. The observer's perceptions and expectations turn waves into solids.

The experiments demonstrated that the way the particles form is directly influenced by our perceptions and expectations of reality. These are, of course, influenced by our belief patterns, life experiences and cultural ideas.

Everything we perceive as "reality" is impacted by our thoughts, perceptions and expectations, which relate to past circumstances and projections of the future.

Therefore, by altering our perceptions and observations, we can alter the way form generates. For instance, scientific research has shown that people with multiple personality disorders can change their physical appearance up to ten times per hour. These shifts can include a change in eye colour, skin complexion, and the appearance of marks on the body. The momentary loss of self and the ability to firmly believe that their personalities have different features allows them to manifest these changes.

This helps us understand that transformation can occur when we are willing to step out of the illusionary realm.

Nils Bohr's Copenhagen interpretation also claimed that it is the consciousness of an intelligent observer that brings it to manifestation in the local realm.

Reality doesn't always match our perception. Much of our idea of reality is based on an illusionary image that can shift if our perception changes.

This leads to a concept I learned from Kenneth Ray Stubbs relating to the relationship between intensity and consciousness.

Intensity refers to energy, the non-local field of frequency waves behind all existence.

Consciousness is the container. It is the set of knowledge, wisdom, perceptions and expectations that brings these non-local wave frequencies into form.

The world needs both intensity and consciousness to exist. Intensity is the Source of all life; consciousness gives it form.

Without intensity, nothing could exist. Without consciousness, the power of intensity would have no way to ever manifest. A poet's inspiration, for instance, would be lost and dissolve into inconsequence if the words to express and organise it didn't exist. Mother nature's vision for a fine red rose would not come into form if there wasn't earth, sun and water to help it grow.

## Source

The concepts of local and non-local lead us to an even more intrinsic and abstract idea: Source.

I see Source as a space of oneness from which all life emerges and into which all life dissolves. It is the eternal origin of all life and the great void of death. It is the unknown which is the all-knowing.

Kenneth Ray Stubbs defined Source as undifferentiated light and pure energy. Because it is undifferentiated, it is oneness, the root of all, where everything meets. Everything originates there.

While Source could be considered part of the non-local, it isn't. It exists beyond it. This is because the non-local inevitably exists in a polarity (i.e., non-local vs local). Source, as oneness itself, exists beyond all polarity.

## The 5 planes of existence

According to Stubbs, our local and non-local universe comprises five planes. When I had previously heard of planes or dimensions, they always felt abstract. It felt like accessing them would require me to explode into space or shoot across a dark, starry galaxy. With time, I learned instead that these planes and dimensions are actually types of energy that are fully accessible to us. They exist within us. What differentiates each plane is how dense the energy is. The 5 planes exist sequentially, ordered from most dense to least dense. The most dense energy is that which is linked to solid form. The least dense energy is that which is linked to Source.

Energies closer to Source are more intrinsic, elemental and inherent to existence. The energy that is densest is the one we experience in physical form (the local) that we can feel, touch and measure. It is the one we experience as we press the hard stone, or hear the yellow lemon thump as it falls from the tree.

It is called live energy, the energy of the molecules and atoms that compose our "reality." Density refers to solidity and also to organisation. The more dense an energy is, the more it is organised in a way that makes sense (e.g., the atoms and molecules that organise into the skin of a lemon.)

The least dense types of energy are further away from form and closest to Source, which is completely formless. The less dense an energy is, the more chaotic it is (i.e., the energy of Source).

Then, there is Source.

**Pure energy (Source):**

It's the primordial undifferentiated essence of our existence. It's the essence of everything. It is nothing, void. Pure energy has no vibratory beingness. It's just a field of undifferentiated white light.

There are five planes in total. Four are non-local, and one is local. The first plane is local. The 2nd to 5th planes are non-local.

Source, the field of pure energy, is not considered a plane because planes require differentiation, which exists in polarity and division. As oneness, Source is beyond polarity and division.

If this all feels confusing, that is fine. There is no need to grasp the specifics of each plane. We simply need to know that each represents a different density level, and that the densest is closest to form and the least dense is closest to the Source.

## How things come into form

As we dig deeper into the local and non-local, the world of energy and the world of form, we start to get some valuable insights into the important process that links the two: the process that brings the formless to form.

## Bohm's theory of form generation

According to 19th-century scientist David Bohm, the universe is one interconnected whole, a holographically interlinked energy network. Our reality originates as something in two dimensions that unfolds into three dimensions.

The physical part of the universe, which is three-dimensional, is impermanent and fully dependent, moment by moment, on the energy emerging from the non-local energy-verse, which is two-dimensional.

We exist in both realms, and there is a continuous relationship between the two.

**String theory**

String theory, first developed by scientist Gabriele
Veneziano, speaks of a vast, unseen, all-pervading realm that
interpenetrates the universe at every point. This realm is filled
with tiny strings and rings of pure energy so small they can't
be measured by human-made instruments. In terms of scale,
these strings and rings are to the nucleus of an atom what the
nucleus of an atom is to the human body.

According to string theory, everything in the universe arises
from this two-dimensional ocean of tiny rings and strings of
vibrating energy. This forms all matter, all measurable energy,
all gravity, and even space itself. The physical world is a tiny
byproduct of a massive 'energy-verse.'

For reasons that will become clearer later in this book, it
is important to note that how each string or ring vibrates
determines how it manifests into solid form. The way an
element vibrates makes it more solid or soft or look one way
or another. We will see later that this is the basis of how the
practice of energy merging can support transformation.

## We are energetic systems

Anything we perceive as form is actually an energetic system made of energy frequencies that have gathered at a specific time and place to respond to a particular set of circumstances.

Every energetic system that comes into form first originates in an unseen realm of pure energy which is made of strings and rings.

While Kenneth Ray Stubbs was not a scientist, his teachings on shamanism and energy work included a theory which explains how we come into form inspired by his time spent with Buddhist rinpoches and Native American shamans. His teachings also often came in the form of downloads he verified using pendulum dowsing, usually verified and confirmed by a professional dowser.

Although not based on science, his theories were interestingly aligned with string theory and Bohm's theory, which I had discovered during our time together.

## Form journeys through the five planes

You previously read about these five planes, which are five types of energy. Below is a summary of the five planes and the journey the frequencies take through them.

### 5th plane - Source energy:
Source energy is the highest form of energy, and it begins to differentiate into individual frequencies.

### 4th plane - Life-force energy:
This plane is where energy begins to exist. With it, intensity

and consciousness begin to become differentiated, and polarisation begins.

### 3rd Plane - Light energy:
This plane is the one in which intensity and consciousness begin to interact to create our form-based reality, a vibratory existence.

### 2nd Plane - Elemental energy:
This plane is the one in which our solid reality begins to be built.

### 1st Plane - Live energy:
This is the plane in which our solid reality exists. It is made of atoms and molecules, which are made up of frequency patterns.

The journey has 3 main stages:
1- Individual frequencies differentiate
2- Frequencies become energy patterns
3- Energy patterns then become energetic abilities and structures

## 1- Individual frequencies differentiate

Everything in existence is a manifestation of vibrations. Every physical object, living being, emotion, issue or pattern we can experience first originates in the realm of Source.

From there, it manifests in the fifth plane. While the realm of Source is simply undifferentiated energy, energy begins to differentiate into individual frequencies in the fifth plane. A frequency is the smallest measurable unit of energy.

Frequencies are the basis of everything in existence. They are barely perceivable as they are the size of a fraction of an atom.

From this fifth plane, it then manifests across all the next planes before finally reaching the first plane of live energy, the "solid and dense" world in which we live.

In sum, everything that comes into form first originates in Source and will move through the five planes before it can be felt in form in the first plane.

If we could see a frequency, they would look like a tiny fragment of a small line of string. They are the ring or the string in the vast field defined in String theory. In the process of generation of form, frequency is the most primordial element.

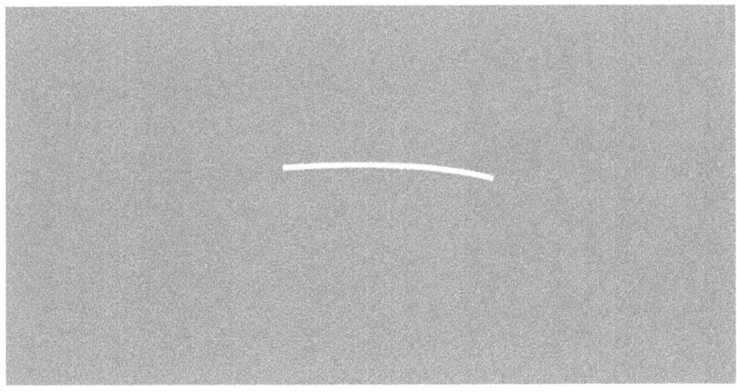

**1.1 - Indidvidual frequencies resemble a tiny fragment of a small line of string.**

## 2- Frequencies become frequency patterns

As frequencies develop, they become frequency patterns. A frequency pattern can be visualised as a line larger than the individual frequency. These then become energetic patterns. Energetic patterns then combine together to create energetic systems. Energetic systems are a combination of energetic patterns which have come together to become a being.  Some beings have consciousness (such as humans) some beings do not (such as "elements forms" like lakes, rocks, trees, etc.).

## 3- Energy patterns then become energetic abilities and structures

Energetic patterns, as they develop, become energetic structures and abilities. Our consciousness affects how these energetic patterns and abilities vibrate, therefore affecting how they are perceived in form.

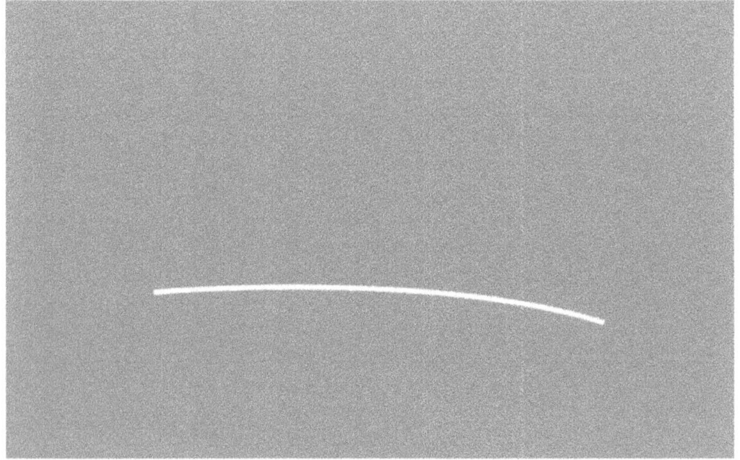

**1.2 - Frequency patterns resemble a small line,
larger than the individual frequency.**

As energetic abilities develop, they create a shape known as a whirling vortex sphere tunnel. If we could see these, they would look like a line with a spiral surrounding it. These are created by combinations of frequencies.

Our energetic abilities and structures play a key role in our energetic development and our ability for energy merging. We will explore this further in a later chapter.

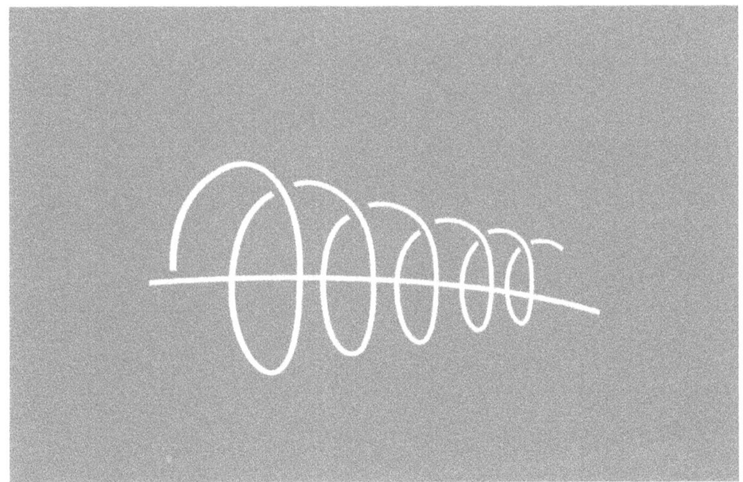

**1.3 - Energetic abilities resemble a line with a spiral surrounding it**

"The first gulp from the glass of natural science will turn you
into an atheist.
But at the bottom of the glass, God is waiting for you. ."

- **Werner Heisenberg**

# 2

# ONENESS

Congratulations on getting through the most theoretical and technical part of this book. While it may have been dense and complex, the key learning comes from understanding that we are all made of interpenetrating vibrating frequency waves. This learning is mainly significant because it demonstrates our innate ability for oneness. We are all inherently whole beings, connected to each other and everything in existence. This ability for oneness is the basis of the energy merging practice.

**What is oneness?**

First, it's important to acknowledge that any attempts to describe oneness through words will inevitably fall short. The true knowingness of oneness can only happen somatically (in the body) and energetically. Still, I will attempt to convey its meaning through words.

Oneness is a state of deep connection and resonance that transcends all limitations and connects us to the infinite. In oneness, I know I am one with every human being, every star in the sky, every blade of grass or grain of salt. The waves that ripple across our oceans also ripple across me, and the fires that burn through our forests and within our volcanoes burn through and within me, too.

In oneness, we are beyond anything that makes sense to the mind, beyond the organised systems of time and space. We are part of an eternal continuum that links everything that exists today, has existed in the past and will exist in the future. Traditional ideas of timelines no longer make sense.

Oneness involves a return to the only place where all is one: to Source, the origin of our existence. We return to the least dense, "pure energy," where nothing is differentiated. It is the field of chaos from which all life emerges and into which it will eventually dissolve. It is a point of complete neutrality beyond any duality and polarity, where heaven meets earth, death is birth, night is day, and dark is light. In oneness, we go from being simple humans to being the force that has created all humans.

## The experience of oneness

A good example of a oneness experience can be found in the book My Stroke Of Insight in which Dr Jill Bolte Taylor, an American neuroanatomist and researcher, describes an experience of observing herself having a stroke.

Her mind dissolved; she could no longer walk, talk, read, write, remember who she was, nor understand words spoken to her. When she attempted to dial the phone to call for help, she couldn't make sense of numbers or letters. She also couldn't distinguish where her fingers ended and the keypad began. She felt her body dissolve into the world around her and no longer was limited by it. Everything was becoming one. The left side of the brain, which relates to logic, rationality, and understanding of time and space, went offline. This is the same part of our brain that clings to the patterns and stories of the past, which limit our sense of self. The part that remained active is the part that doesn't see limits. It is beyond division and connected to oneness.

She found herself experiencing a state she described as complete euphoria and Nirvana. She felt suspended in a realm beyond her past, beyond any stories, narratives or baggage which had limited or plagued her life until that point.

While she eventually had to undergo surgery and a gruelling rehabilitation process, what she learned from the experience changed her life:

Oneness is always within our reach if we choose to move beyond what divides us.

Hearing a scientist share this type of experience enabled me to understand some of the mechanics behind oneness and make sense of something that is almost impossible to explain.

As far as science is concerned, oneness relates to our connection to the non-local, holographic field. We connect to the one force behind the creation of all existence; the force that powers a tornado, that opens the petals of a flower, that wriggles our fingers and toes and can spontaneously arch our back in ecstasy when we experience an orgasm.

**Oneness and the orgasm**

According to Kenneth Ray Stubbs, the only way to achieve oneness which is available to every human indiscriminately, is through the orgasm. When we are in orgasm, three things happen: we automatically become one with whoever we are with at the time, we automatically get access to more energy, and we connect to the less dense energies of the non-local.  In sum, when we are in orgasm, we have the ability to be one with the entire universe.

## The healing oneness

So what makes connecting to oneness so healing?

The philosopher Plato spoke about oneness as the eternal now where we can access all the wisdom and beauty of the universe. He spoke of it as the only universal absolute truth. Everything that keeps us from it is an illusion, a lie.

We, like everything in existence, came from oneness. Returning to oneness allows us to return to our truth and transcend the illusions that have shown up along the way that have shaped and limited us. The more time we spend in oneness, the more our connection to Source develops. We discover the parts of ourselves that exist beyond the patterns and stories that normally limit us. Our truth can unfold. Being in oneness allows us to be all we can be from a physical, emotional, energetic and spiritual point of view.

When we are in oneness, we vibrate like Source and everything in existence. How frequencies vibrate directly affects how an energy system manifests into form. Therefore, how we vibrate directly affects who we are in the world.

When two systems connect, they vibrate like each other. When we are in oneness with Source, we vibrate like Source and all of existence.

**Source has no problems.**

Anything we consider problematic or dissonant results from a polarity, such as good or bad, right or wrong, dark or light, etc., it has come out of oneness and wholeness.

As Source is beyond polarity, it is inevitably neutral. Connecting to Source and finding this oneness will allow us to move beyond polarity and find neutrality. Similarly to neuroanatomist Jill Bolte Taylor, when we are in oneness, we operate in a space beyond the trauma, circumstances and narratives of the past that have limited us. The more time we spend in that space, the less bound we are by these limitations, and the more transformation and healing can occur.

**What has disconnected?**

An exploration of oneness will inevitably show us all the aspects of ourselves that are not in oneness, that have been separated.

Everything that challenges us, whether an emotional issue, a physiological or health issue, a financial issue, etc., is the result of a disconnection. This is because we come from oneness, and all is unified and well in oneness. Therefore, something that challenges us inevitably relates to a disconnection from oneness.

These challenges also relate to polarities, such as good vs. bad, right vs. wrong, pain vs. pleasure, and abundant vs. scarce. In oneness, none of these polarities exist.

This division is an illusion. All of existence is made of patterns which are all interconnected. Separation is merely a perception that exists at the level of form and is illusionary.

There are three levels of division.

The first relates to the illusion of separation first occurs through the process of differentiation and individuation, which occurs naturally as we physically incarnate in human form. At a universal level, all of our energetic bodies flow around the universe freely. Eventually, an energy body will choose to incarnate into physical form.

A sperm and an egg meet and create a fertilised egg cell. This cell multiplies and expands through mitosis, and the embryo forms. For the first few days of this formation, the embryo is a blastocyst, merely a ball of water floating in water. A thin layer called the Zona pellucida separates the blastocyst from the world outside of it. For this short period, the cell appears to be completely isolated but is connected to oneness and all of existence. It has access to all existence within it.

When the Zona pellucida hatches on day 5 or 6, implantation begins, a process by which the embryo is nourished from the uterine wall. We begin to become dependent on the world around us for survival, which inevitably affects our connection to the self.

We become human beings with emotional bodies which can confuse things. Over-identification with emotions can make it more difficult to connect to more primordial energies.

The second relates to collective ideas. As we engage with life, we are inevitably shaped and influenced by the division in our culture. We are exposed to the limitations imposed by thousands of years of collective conditioning, illusionary perspectives and deeply embedded belief systems.

The third relates to our own personal experience of life. In addition to these collective distortions, there are individual ones specific to each of us. Each of us will inevitably face a series of circumstances that will shape and affect us, which are different to those experienced by others.

Division often occurs when we encounter situations in which we feel threatened. We inevitably create defense mechanisms to protect ourselves. While protection can be useful, it also creates division. This division is expressed in our physical body and will, consequentially, also exist in our energy body.

## Body Armouring

Body armouring is an example of this. It refers to the unconscious muscular tensions and patterns that develop in response to emotional and psychological experiences as we go through life intending to survive. These tensions create a physical armour that shields us from the perceived threat. While this armour protects us, it also restricts our ability to be in oneness and wholeness in the body.

A body that is in oneness supports a consciousness being in oneness. Therefore, when a body cannot be in oneness, it is also harder for our consciousness to be in oneness.

Responses like body armouring enable us to navigate life in survival mode. Muscle tension arises as a way to block or suppress emotional expression. People may tense their shoulders, jaw, or chest to suppress anger, fear, or sadness.

The body can also tighten in preparation for physical defense (fight) or escape (flight). When this state is sustained, it becomes chronic body armouring.

While it creates a buffer against intense feelings and stressors, it also buffers resources and pleasure, including the energy of Source (our greatest resource).

**Nervous system responses**

Over time, body armouring can lead the autonomic nervous system to become dysregulated.

The autonomic nervous system (ANS) is the part of the nervous system that regulates involuntary physiological functions such as heart rate, digestion, respiration, and the fight-or-flight response. It comprises two main branches:

Sympathetic Nervous System (SNS): Activates the body's fight-or-flight response to stress or danger.

Parasympathetic Nervous System (PNS): Activates the body's freeze response to stress and danger. It also promotes rest, relaxation, and recovery by slowing down bodily functions after the threat has passed, helping to restore balance.

Continued experiences of perceived threat lead to the sympathetic nervous system staying activated for long periods, making the body feel constantly prepared for fight or flight. This constant activation can result in chronic muscle tension or body armouring. The body stays in a high-alert state, leading to issues like anxiety, poor sleep, digestive problems, and even cardiovascular issues.

In some cases, the body might experience a parasympathetic shutdown in which the body shuts down emotionally or physically as a survival mechanism, causing a freeze response.

Body armouring can arise as part of this "freeze" response, where tension locks into specific muscle groups.

## The HPA axis

The HPA axis is another human function that supports us in responding to threats and can inhibit our ability to be in oneness or wholeness.

It is a complex set of interactions among three key endocrine glands:

Hypothalamus: Located in the brain.
Pituitary Gland: also located in the brain.
Adrenal Glands: Located on top of the kidneys.

When the body perceives stress, the HPA axis is activated. The hypothalamus releases hormones, triggering the pituitary gland to release hormones too. This release stimulates the adrenal glands to release cortisol, which prepares the body for a "fight-or-flight" response by increasing blood sugar, suppressing the immune system, and redirecting energy to critical functions like muscles and brain activity.

The HPA axis regulates many of the body's functions, including stress responses, immune reactions, digestion, mood, and energy levels.

When the HPA axis is frequently activated due to continuously experiencing exposure to threats, the body forms stress-related behaviour patterns. The HPA axis might become overly sensitive and over reactive. Fight, flight or freeze responses can arise even as reactions to minor stressors.

A person may also develop avoidance patterns to reduce HPA activation, such as avoiding social situations. Repeated activation of the HPA axis can contribute to the development of compulsive behaviours (e.g., overeating, substance abuse) as a way to cope with stress and regulate the emotional state.

I tend to like to illustrate this with the following example. Imagine a house gets robbed and the owners, in order to keep it safe, install a super high-tech alarm system. Perhaps this system is so sophisticated that if a butterfly were to land on the window sill it would set the alarm off. While the alarm is effectively doing its job, keeping the house safe from potential robbery, it is also creating division from other elements and beings which do not pose a real threat, such as a butterfly.

**Associative learning**

The HPA axis is also involved in associative learning. The body and brain learn to associate specific stimuli with stress. For example, if a person has been abandoned by their father, the brain can create a link between the significant masculine figure and the fear of abandonment. The activation of the HPA axis might then be heightened when they enter a relationship with a man in the future. They might fear that this male figure they have forged a bond with might abandon them, similar to the way their father abandoned them in the past.

These learned associations can turn into patterned behaviours, where the individual reacts to the environment in predictable ways—for example, feeling anxious or stressed when they begin to date, even if no immediate threat is present. These patterned behaviours are linked to the intelligent observer and consciousness concepts, which we explored in Chapter 1. In the double-slit experiment, the way the photons projected on the back panel varied depending on whether or not there was a sensor. The sensor had been placed by a scientist who had specific expectations about how the photons would project.

Our consciousness and expectations, shaped by our patterns and history, affect how energy vibrates. The way things vibrate affects the way they come into form. Therefore, our expectations based on associative learning will affect the way frequencies vibrate. This will affect the way we show up in the world and face situations, affecting their outcome.

**Energetic suppression and un-suppression**

Like Jill Bolte Taylor having a oneness experience as she had her stroke, when we are in oneness, we are in a space that is beyond our patterns, stories, trauma and the impact of the circumstances of the past.

The HPA axis, the body armouring, and the ANS responses all create division, which exists in the body and is reflected as suppression of the energy patterns in the energy body. Energy merging can be a way to address these distortions, which are based in division.

Everything in the local world of form has a blueprint in the non-local energetic realm. When something is dissonant or problematic, it also exists energetically as well. Anything dissonant, such as emotional blocks, physical pains, trauma, or other disruptions, also exist non-locally in our energy bodies. They are seen as suppression in our energetic patterns.

Connecting to Source allows these to become un-suppressed.

**This happens through a process of energy merging.**

The energy of Source is the least suppressed and least dense. When we connect to Source, these suppressed energy patterns vibrate like Source. As a result, they become unsuppressed, and the impact can be felt in the local world of form. Healing and transformation occur.

The moment a change happens in the non-local is the exact moment it manifests in our local physical world. This energetic unsuppression shows up as a shift in our daily experience.

This is transformation

I define transformation as a return to truth. Things can change in many ways, but transformation is more than change. When life transforms, it returns to its most truthful expression, less affected by circumstances, beliefs, patterns and narratives that are illusionary.

**Energy merging and transmission**

In this process of connection to Source, transmission takes place. Transmission is a communication between two energetic systems that is beyond the understanding of the mind. While we can't understand it or explain it with words, we know it yields an impact.

In this case, the human being connecting to Source is one energetic system, and Source is the other.

In this process, two things happen as they connect:
1- The two systems vibrate like each other.
2- The two systems have access to the same energy.

## 1- The two systems vibrate like each other.

As we are made of frequencies vibrating, we are energetic systems vibrating to a specific rhythm that will change depending on what we connect to. A shift therefore happens through energetic merging where two (or more) energetic systems function as one. As the two systems connect to each other and merge into one system, they begin to vibrate like each other. When the way we vibrate changes, we change.

In science, this process is explained through the concept of entrainment. As energetic systems, we are made of frequencies that oscillate and are in constant movement. Systems that oscillate synchronise with each other when they come together. The movement of one system will change to match the movement of the other system. This process is known as entrainment.

We can imagine this process by visualising a set of pendulum clocks hanging on a wall beside each other. Even if we were to intentionally set them to swing to different rhythms, they would eventually meet and swing to the same rhythm.

The same is true of human heart rates. During emotional conversations, dinner, sex or other social activities, our heartbeats synchronise.

Another commonly known example of entrainment is the menstrual cycle. Women who spend significant time together will find their menstrual cycles entrain, causing them to synchronise over time. The same is, therefore, true for our energetic resources.

**2- The two systems have access to the same energy.**

When two systems merge into one system together, they have access to the same energy. The energy that is available to one becomes available to the other. Therefore, they both have access to more energy.

This is what happens when two beings vibrate like each other. When they are in oneness together, a sharing of energy takes place. The energy available to one being becomes available to both. As a result of this, transmission takes place.

This sharing of energy is not about one system transferring or giving energy to another system. It's about two systems connecting and merging. In that connected space, the access to energy that exists for one system awakens within the other.

When a being with suppressed energetic patterns connects to Source and, as a result, experiences un-suppression, this is transmission. A sharing of energy has taken place between two systems and yielded an impact.

**Energetic development is necessary.**

Achieving this requires some abilities that are often either dormant or compromised. For one energetic system to merge into oneness with another, it needs to be able to vibrate like it. To be one with all of existence, we need to vibrate like all of existence. This means we must be able to vibrate like the five energy planes. This requires a process of development to take place. We will explore this process more deeply in chapter 4.

"We are beginning to see the entire universe as a holographically interlinked network of energy and information, organically whole and self referential at all scales of its existence. We, and all things in the universe, are non-locally connected with each other and with all other things in ways that are unfettered by the hitherto known limitations of space and time."

- Ervin Laszlo -"Cosmos: A Co-Creator's Guide to the Whole-World" (2010)

3

# THE ENERGY BEING: THE SHAMAN AND THE SACRED PROSTITUTE

What would it be like if humans could exist in constant engagement with Source? How would we live if we could have continuous access to healing resources at any time, not just in orgasm?

Indeed, some people seem to have been born with special superpowers and live more like deities embodied in human form rather than as "normal" humans. Perhaps the Dalai Lama or a child chosen at three years old to be the rinpoche of a monastery in Kathmandu were born with these abilities. They might appear to live with greater ease or connect to a "greater power" more effortlessly and easily than the rest of us.

However, the connection to Source is intrinsic to all of us and is not a privilege reserved for a chosen few. If, according to quantum physics, the universe and all of existence are composed of energy at 99.99%, this also applies to humans.

If the universe consists of two interconnected, interwoven parts constantly in dialogue, and all life forms, conscious or not, exist in both, this is true of us as well.

Therefore, the ability to cross over from the local realm of form into the vast formless non-local expanse belongs to us, too. However, the level of development of this connection and the ability to access, experience, and resource it vary from person to person.

Some beings benefit from a high level of energetic development and have access to the resources of oneness and Source at all times, unlike most humans who only have access to them during orgasms.

I call them energy beings.

An energy being is a highly energetically developed person. As a result, they have access to more energy than the average human, which they can use to support their transformation and development and that of others. They often do so simply by the power of their presence.

What makes people like the Dalai Lama or these other archetypes so powerful is not what they do in the world but who they are. It is not about the books they write or speeches they give, but rather how we feel while in their presence.

In the introduction, I mentioned that the shamanic mission in Brazil allowed us to reconnect to a premise that existed in ancient civilisations: that humans could bring impact and transformation to others simply by the power of their presence. I also mentioned how timely it was that I met Stubbs at the tail-end of that very journey.

When I first connected with Stubbs, what struck me was not the fact that he had authored so many best-selling books that had been translated and used in training courses around the world or the fact that he had been one of the forefathers of

Tantra in the West, leading the way since the early 1970s. It was the power of his presence. Merely connecting with him for a quick thirty-second video chat impacted me like an experience at a sacred temple. This is the power of the energy being.

The Indian spiritual leader Mata Amritanandamayi, also known as Amma, is an example of this. Known as "the hugging saint," Amma travels the world giving hugs to thousands of people who queue up for hours outside packed stadiums to wait for her. But it is not just a hug. Interacting with Amma is considered a deep spiritual experience that can enhance your life. At the time of writing this book, more than 34 million people have received hugs from her.

This can be seen as a modern interpretation of the biblical stories of Jesus and other saints. We have read of Jesus walking through crowds of people, bringing impact and healing simply with his presence. Many would gather to simply clutch his robe as he passed by, knowing that this would somehow transmit a power that would be healing and transformative.

I remember witnessing scenes like this when I visited Bethlehem, specifically at the church built on the spot where Jesus was supposedly born. Crowds queued for hours to touch the stone that rested in its basement. They would huddle around the stone, rubbing it with tissues to attempt to take away some of the healing power.

The story of Jesus Christ is meant to show us the potential of who we could be if we awakened dormant powers.

He is a human being created in the image of God, who is seen as the creator and, therefore, the Source of all.

To be in oneness, we must be able to vibrate like all of existence. God, as the creator of all, could be seen as a being that could vibrate like everything in existence.

What is experienced in the clutch of Jesus' robe or a hug with Amma is transmission. Both Jesus and Amma must be able to transmit energetically to others. This means they have access to a certain power and have the ability to share it with others. Simply through the power of their presence, a communication occurs between them and the other energetic system (i.e., human being) that is beyond the understanding of the mind and yields impact.

As a side note, I highly recommend the book "Resurrecting Jesus" by author and speaker Adyashanti. It draws links between the archetypes portrayed in the Bible and characters that could exist in our modern context. I sense that Adyashanti is one of these very highly developed beings that Selbie was writing about, almost like a saint, in a modern-day context.

## The shaman and the sacred prostitute

The two archetypes I most often use to portray the concept of the energy being are the shaman and the sacred prostitute.

## The shaman

A shaman is a bridge to the unseen, the formless and the non-local. A shaman is an energy being so developed that merely their presence, focus and attention are enough to support transformation in others. The shaman, therefore, teaches by transmission.

Sometimes they say nothing and appear to be doing nothing at all. Other times they might use costumes, props, or more intricate activities we often associate with shamanism. But a true shaman does not need them.

The etymology of shamanism is rooted in the word šamán, which comes from the Manchu-Tungus languages in Siberia and northern Asia and means "to know." The shaman is "the one who knows." This knowingness, however, is not one of knowledge in terms of wisdom and information, as we might think. It refers to a knowingness of the non-local, the unseen. This energetic knowingness refers to the ability to vibrate like all of existence, all the planes of the non-local.

If a shaman develops this strong connection to the non-local, which contains the blueprint behind everything, they have access to a realm where a change in vibration can occur. This will inevitably bring about a change in the local world of form.

It is important to mention that I arrived at this definition of a shaman through research and mentorship by Ray Stubbs. It might differ from other ideas, often linking shamans to plant medicine or as connectors to the spirit world.

In my time with Ray Stubbs, I learned that there are three types of shamans.

- The traditional shaman
- The vibrational shaman
- The energy shaman

## The traditional shaman

The traditional shaman might generally fit our conventional idea of a shaman. They might live in a tribe in Peru or Mongolia or be part of a Native American tribe. They might conduct traditional ceremonies influenced by lineage, which may or may not include plant medicine.

## The vibrational shaman

The vibrational shaman is connected to similar philosophies as the traditional shaman but lives in the West and, therefore, is more integrated into our culture. They connect to the spirit world as a way of connecting to Source. Shamans who conduct plant medicine ceremonies in the West would belong to this category.

## The energy shaman

The energy shaman is not connected to the spirit world but connects to the Source in other, more direct ways. They support others by sharing that connection with them. This third type of shaman is an energy being; they teach by transmission.

When my journey to shamanism began in 2015, I visualised the shaman as an elder with long hair and a beard, wearing many large necklaces and playing the drum. They would chant and perform intricate theatrical ceremonies in ornate settings, such as a fully decorated yurt in nature.

In contrast, shamans such as Stubbs and those with whom I shared the journeys in Brazil appeared like "normal folk." You wouldn't bat an eyelid if you saw them in a supermarket.

I learned that even if a shaman performs apparently complex and theatrical ceremonies, their power lies elsewhere. It lies in the transmission, the unseen communication behind the ceremony, or that can be experienced alongside it.

The ceremony can have value because it can keep our attention and offer the mind a point of focus so that we can trust that something is taking place.

A good example of this is the 2009 movie The Horse Boy, directed by Michael O. Scott. It tells the story of a family with an autistic child who flies to Mongolia to attempt to find healing after the Western medical system seemed to fall short. The family decides to visit many shamans and experience various ceremonies which yield little or no results. At the end of the journey, they encounter a last shaman. This one stands very still, appearing to do very little as he gently waves an incense burner.

The child's tantrum calmed when faced with this shaman and his stillness. In the following days, the parents were stunned by the child's behaviour, which had been visibly altered. To the outside spectator, it would appear as if the shaman had done nothing.  It was, in fact, the power of an unseen transmission that enabled the shift.

I remember a similar experience when I attended a gathering with a Siberian shaman in a retreat house in the woods between Germany and the Netherlands. He first mumbled a few words about attachments, nothing more than what I'd already heard Buddhists say, before telling us to lie down while he played his drum for about eleven minutes.

As soon as he started playing, I felt transported into an altered state. Everything dissolved, and I lost all notions of time and space.

That night, I experienced a series of vivid lucid dreams, which I know is a sign that the conscious and unconscious spaces had been bridged. Coincidentally, within two weeks of that experience, I met the partner with whom I would have my next significant relationship.

Like the shaman in the Horse Boy documentary, the shaman did very little during the ceremony. However, by connecting with the shaman, I experienced a transmission of energy that supported the awakening of a previously dormant resource within me. As a result of awakening this resource, I found myself engaging differently with this new partner than I would have with previous ones, leading us to create a deep and lasting connection.

## The sacred prostitute

The second archetype I like to refer to when speaking of the energy being is the sacred prostitute. Just by the name, this archetype might feel at odds with the other energy beings I mentioned so far.

The two words, when combined, might even feel radical and contradictory. "Sacred" suggests a connection to the divine spirit, while "prostitute" suggests transgression, sin, and the breaking of commandments. Combined, they create a whole new meaning that is provocative and radical.

Herodotus first used the term in the 5th century BC to refer to an archetype in various cultures and civilisations.

Jungian analyst Nancy Qualls-Corbett wrote extensively about this archetype in her book The Sacred Prostitute: Eternal Aspect Of The Feminine.

In Ancient Greece, Egypt, Jerusalem, Sumer, etc., the sacred prostitute was known as the physical embodiment of the goddesses of fertility and sexuality, such as Aphrodite, Hathor, Astarte, Inanna, etc.

She was a temple priestess who helped facilitate transformation through sexuality in these various cultures. Worshipers would visit them, seeking healing and abundance. She would receive offerings in exchange for sex and lovemaking. Unlike in our usual images of prostitution, they weren't selling a sexual act as a service, but rather a healing process.

Notions of sex also expanded beyond those that are common to us today, which generally refer to the rubbing together of organs and eventually reaching an orgasmic climax. Sex was an act of energies merging that would connect us to Source. As sexual energy rises in the body, it leads us to altered states of awareness. These acts connected us to the archetypal world, which connected us to the spirit world, allowing healing to occur.

The sacred prostitute supported society in times of crisis. According to Nancy Qualls-Corbet, they would support the warriors and politicians in transmuting the PTSD experienced through the horrors of war. The affected man would visit the sacred prostitute in her chamber, and she would bathe, feed, massage, and eventually make love to him. Through a sacred act of sex, she would draw the energy of the horrors of war from the men's bodies through their sperm and transmute it so they no longer carried it and wouldn't take it home to their families or into society.

But as powerful as all those actions are, they are probably, on their own, not effective enough to wash away PTSD and the horrors of war in such a short time.

Another unseen process was also taking place: a process of energy merging related to the sacred prostitute's own energetic development.

It was well known that the sacred prostitute was not only a sex worker but also a bridge to the healing power of Source and the non-local. By connecting (or merging) with the non-local, her own energetic structures would have been developed, allowing her a more direct connection to oneness and Source that she could share with others when sharing an intimate space of presence.

Also, the fact that there was ejaculation underscores the fact that an orgasm had taken place. As the pair experienced an orgasm together, an act of merging took place between the two, leading to them being one energetically together. As a result, a sharing of energetic resources could take place.

Although they might all appear different, what unites a shaman, a rinpoche, the Dalai Lama, or a sacred prostitute is their common ability to impact others through the power of their energy and presence. Beyond all the differentiated archetypes, they are all energy beings. However, these abilities exist in each of us to varying degrees and can always be developed further.

**The human being**

The human being is an aggregate of an energy field connected to everything in existence. Like everything, it has a local expression, limited by form, and a non-local expression, which is infinite.

The human body is the part of our being that is limited in time and space. It is dense, organised and is only a small part of our whole being. Still, it is much more than we think.

Our body appears dense and solid but is also a gateway to Source and the formless. Every cell has a local existence and a non-local one. The two affect each other and relate directly to each other.

In her book Life On Land, Emilie Conrad, the creator of the

somatic therapy practice Continuum Movement, defines the body in the following way:

"What we call "body" is an open-ended expression of an ongoing universal process that began billions of years ago. It is a system in constant flux, arranging and rearranging, experimenting as new formations come into existence."

Our body is made of interpenetrating wave motions that have stabilised in time in a way that allows us to survive successfully on this planet.

Each being is an energetic system not confined to the physical body we can't see or measure. The physical body is simply where the wave function is densest; therefore, it can be measured, touched and seen.

We've been taught not to trust what we cannot see. Therefore, our perceptions of ourselves seldom expand beyond the physical. Our experience of ourselves as something separate from everything else is an optical delusion of our limited consciousness. In fact, invisible quantum waves are spreading out of each of us and interpenetrating into all organisms. Therefore, we each have the waves of every organism entangled within us and are each supported by the entire universe.

This is the basis of oneness and energy merging.

# 4

# OUR ENERGY BODY

The ability to be in oneness and to merge energetically requires the development of energetic abilities. While some people, like the Dalai Lama or a young rinpoche, might be born with these, most of us need to develop them if we want to yield similar impact. We do so through the development of our energy (holographic) body.

**Our energy body**

Bohm's theory describes the universe as one interconnected whole, a holographically interlinked network of energy. The physical part of the universe is wholly dependent, moment by moment, on the information and energy emerging from the non-local.

This is true of our physical body as well. It is continuously created by the information received from its own energetic template. Our physical body is made of "lower frequency", detectable energies that masquerade as matter. Our energy (holographic) body is made of coordinated energies that vibrate at frequencies impossible for physical instruments to measure or detect.

Our physical bodies are the moment-by-moment result of a process by which non-local energies interact with each other and vibrate in a specific way. The way they vibrate results in our local 3-dimensional body coming to form. The way they vibrate is shaped by various factors, such as consciousness (expectations), entrainment, (the impact of transmission) etc.

Joseph Selbie also speaks of liquid crystal structures that exist within our tissues. These allow the information from our holographic energy template to initiate and coordinate the creation of our physical body. The liquid crystal structures within our tissues phase in and out of quantum coherence, allowing the information from our energy (holographic) body to initiate and coordinate the creation of our physical body.

When we feel the energy of our holographic being, we call it life force energy. When we perceive this energy, our journey of connection to Source begins.

According to Stubbs, the difference between these energy beings who have access to oneness at all times, such as the Dalai Lama, some rinpoches, shamans, sacred prostitutes, etc., and the majority of society is the level of development of our energy (holographic) body. The more developed our energy body is, the more connected we are to Source and the more we can transform.

We saw earlier that we are energetic systems. Like everything in existence, we are composed of energy, more specifically energetic frequencies which combine to create an energetic system that appears to be solid form. Our energy frequencies combine to create frequency patterns which evolve to become energetic structures. These structures, when they develop, become vortices. A vortex is an interface that serves as a bridge between the material world and  Source. Its function is to transform pure energy into a form that can be usable by us. Therefore, our energetic structures allow us to connect to the non-local planes and Source and to be that connecting point for others, too.

Developing these structures is essential to developing the ability to reach oneness. Unless these are developed, the being will only be able to reach oneness through the orgasm.

The chakra system, which we will read more about below, is the most popular example of an energetic structure. Most energetic structures are found in the area of our energetic mid-line, a tube running across the centre of our body that expands above our head and below our feet, or in the centre of our physical body, in the lower belly area below the navel.

The following pages will share the key highlights regarding the 20 human energetic structures. It might appear quite theoretical and dense. It is not crucial to grasp it all to the finest detail. The main aim of this chapter is for us to become aware of the structures that compose our system, and therefore support the development of our energetic body.

**The 20 human energetic structures.**

The human being comprises 20 energetic structures.

The Dalai Lama, certain rinpoches and shamans might be born with these 20 energetic structures fully functioning, which allows them to be more connected to Source.

According to Stubbs, most of us function with only eight structures developed and can develop the other 12 structures.

The eight structures that are active in every human being at birth are the following:

1- Physical body
2- Light body
3- Spirit body
4- Soul body
5- Resonating body
6- Wisdom body
7- Retrieval system
8- Embodying energetic structure

The 12 others which are less commonly developed are the following:

9- The self
10- The shamanic infrastructure
11- The double
12- The Sourcepoint
13- The emanation processing body
14- Intensity body: kundalini
15- Energetic patterns body
16- Skeletal energetic structure

17- Muscular energetic structure

18- Nervous energetic structure

19- Biological synthesis

20- Cellular/nuclear energetic structure

## The Sourcepoint

The Sourcepoint is the most important energetic structure because it serves as a tool for developing other energetic structures.

The Sourcepoint is located in the navel area about 3-4 finger widths beneath the navel and halfway into the depth of the body. It's oval-shaped and the size of a green pea. Unlike the seven main chakras, it's unrelated to a physical part of the human body.

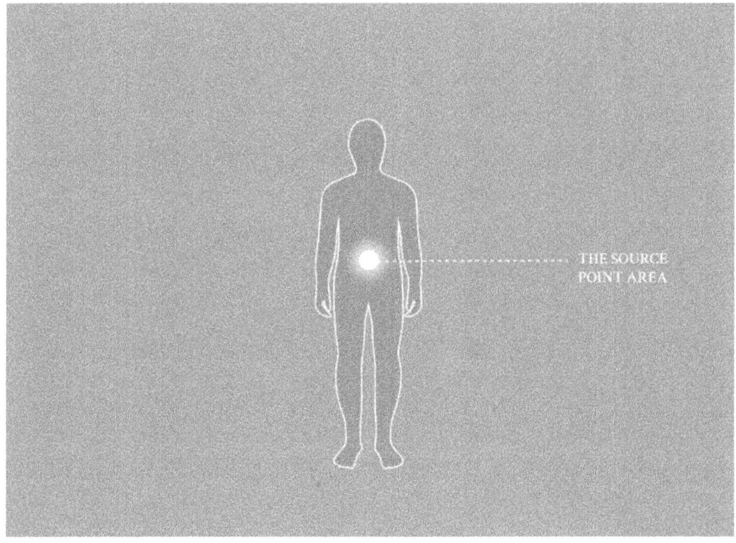


4. 1- The Sourcepoint

The Sourcepoint intensifies the speed of an energetic pattern. An energetic pattern is formed of various energetic frequencies which come together as they develop. Concentrating on the Sourcepoint intentionally therefore brings about an intentional process of energetic intensification.

Other philosophies and practices often associate the lower belly area with the lower tan t'ien. When exploring the Sourcepoint, it can be easy to confuse the two and believe they are the same. The Sourcepoint is a completely separate energetic structure from the tan t'ien. While the Sourcepoint intensifies energetic structures, the tan t'ien is known as for storing energy which can later be used by our being. Ray Stubbs also believed the tan t'ien played a role in distributing energy throughout the light body.

The Sourcepoint can be seen as a microcosm of the macrocosm, a structure in our body that allows us to access more energy by connecting us to the plane of pure energy and Source.

We will later see that the Sourcepoint is also a key element to the energy merging practice.

It plays a key role in generating more energy to develop our energetic structures and holding space for others as facilitators. We will see how the Sourcepoint can allow us to live in the world while connecting to the greater overarching power of Source and pure energy.

**The energy core**

Another one of the most central energetic structures is the

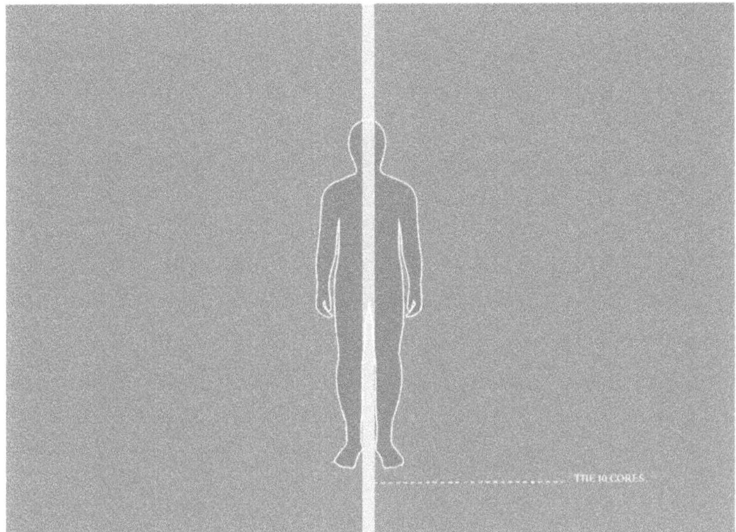


**4. 2- The energy core / 10-core system**

10-core system, also known as the energy core. It consists of 10 strands that form a tube of white light approximately 8cm in diameter.

It runs along the centre of our body, beginning 1.5m above the top of our head and ending 1.5m below our feet. Its function is to allow our body to access energies from Source.

**The chakra system**

The chakra system is the most commonly discussed energetic structure in popular spiritual practices. According to Stubbs, there are seven main chakras within our physical body and three secondary chakras above and below.

Chakras are energy patterns that originally take the shape of a whirling vortex cone. Some will take the shape of two or

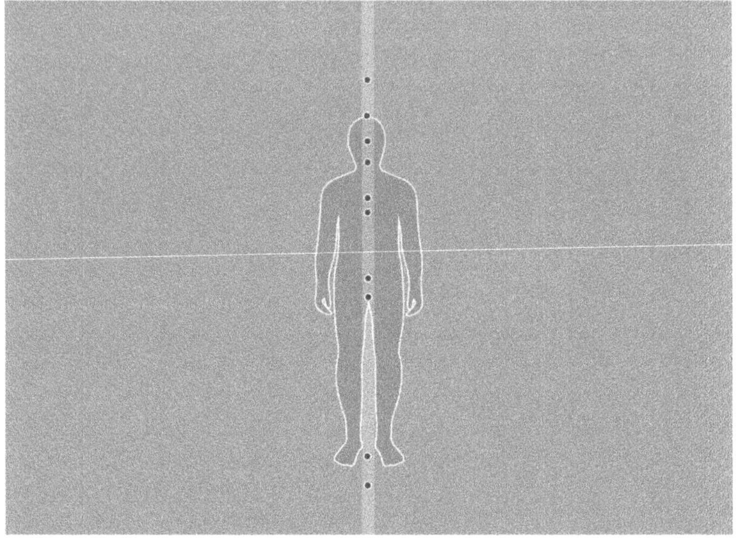

**4. 3- The 10-core system and the chakra system**

three vortex cones as they develop. In a way, the chakras are the digestion system for the other energetic structures.

Each of the seven main chakras relates to a specific body part. Their main function is to transform and transmute physical energy into other forms of energy for the other energetic structures to use.

## The 20 transformation centres

The transformation centres are vortices that exist across the central line of the 10-core system. The 20 transformation centres allow energy to go up and down the 10-core strand. As the energy goes up and down, the energy gets transfered into patterns the human organism can use. The solar plexus makes these energy patterns available to the human system.

The 20 transformation centres are found in the following locations:

1. At the bottom end of the energy field
2. Halfway between the bottom end of the energy field and the bottom of the feet
3. At the bottom of the feet
4. At the knees
5. At the level of the mid-thigh
6. At the perineum
7. Halfway between the Sourcepoint and the perineum
8. At the Sourcepoint
9. At the heart
10. At the throat
11. At the third eye
12. At the top of the head
13. Eight more transformation centres are located above the head.

**Whirling vortex disks**

There are seven whirling vortex disks which are part of the human energetic system. Each of these is in the shape of a torus and transforms and generates pure energy to be used by a different part of our being.

**The light body**

Our light body is an energetic structure that is the same shape as our physical body but expands beyond it. It runs through the physical body, generally through our body's energetic system composed of meridians and energy lines. The size of the light body will vary from person to person, but it usually expands about 30cm around the physical body.

The light body can be seen as the energetic version of the physical body. It is its similar to those an architect creates for a house or a bridge. Working with the light body means we are generally working more intrinsically, connecting more deeply to the origins of who we are. It's, therefore, more directly connected to oneness and Source.

It is the part of Source that gets expressed through each of us, which we can use in the day-to-day. The light body carries pure light energy through our physical body's network of energy channels (meridians and nadis).

I mentioned earlier that challenges and divisive circumstances can often cause suppression which manifests in the energy body. The light body is where this suppression takes place, therefore it is also where it can be unsuppressed and transformed.

## The retrieval system

The retrieval system is a very fine and subtle system between the physical body and the and light body. It's about 2cm (almost 1 inch) thick, begins 1cm below the skin layer, and extends to 1cm outside of the skin layer. Like the light body, it takes the shape of the physical body.

Its main function is to store information as energetic codes, which our being can then engage with and retrieve as needed. The retrieval system is the bridge between the physical body and the light body.

## The spirit body

The spirit body is an oval-shaped energetic system that expands beyond the light body. It stores primordial or elemental energy that has yet to be transformed for use by the system.

For instance, when we are experiencing a transmission, that energy will normally be transformed and used by certain energetic structures. When energy has not yet been transformed, it gets suspended and stored in the spirit body.

The spirit body also works with the emotional energy which is sometimes stuck in the retrieval system resulting in what is considered in Buddhism and Tantra as "attachments."

In the process of having an orgasm, the spirit body works with the light body to unravel some of these emotions. This is why some of us experience powerful emotional releases, which often include crying, when we experience an orgasm.

## The rainbow body

The rainbow body is the 21st energetic structure and encompasses all others. For it to be developed, the other 20 energetic structures have to be developed first.

In Buddhism, the rainbow body is often depicted as a sphere of light highly evolved beings merge into at death. However, Kenneth Ray Stubbs proposed a different perspective. He suggested that the rainbow body is not just a post-mortem phenomenon but a structure that we can actively develop and utilize in our current lives.

He speaks of it as a sphere-shaped vortex structure, which, when developed, offers us continued and constant access to Source and Pure energy as a resource in our daily lives. It is the highest energetic development a human being can reach.

According to Stubbs, some people are born with active rainbow bodies simply because they developed them in past incarnations. They may also have been born with one simply because it was part of their journey to be a rainbow body on earth. This might be the case for people like the superbeings I keep referring to.

For most of us, the path to the rainbow body is within reach. The journey may vary in intensity and rigour depending on the level of development we have achieved in previous lifetimes or even in this lifetime, but it is a journey we can all embark on.

As we have seen, humans are made of two parts that work together to function. The physical body and the energy (holographic) body. When a human has a functioning rainbow body, the two units become one integrated unit.

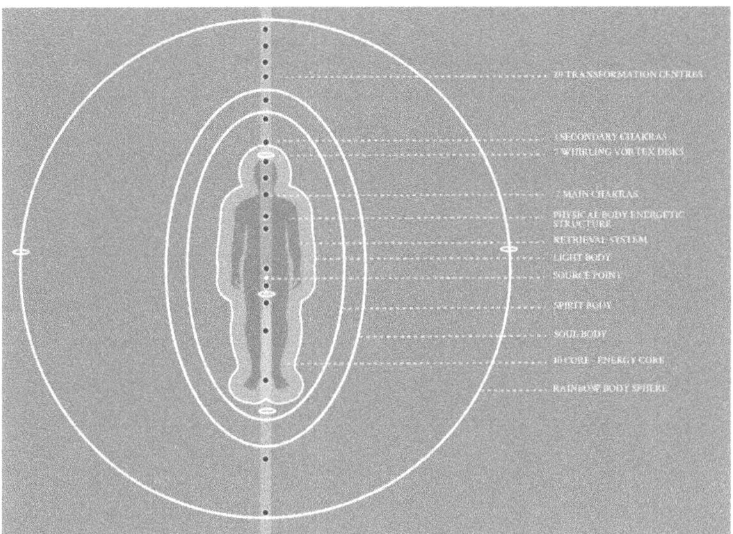



**4. 4- The complete energy body**

If this seems too technical, don't worry—it's not necessary to understand every detail of the energetic structures. However, being aware of the various components that make up our energetic body can help us realize that we are more than we think.

# 5

## ENERGY MERGING:
## AN INTENTIONAL ACT OF
## BEING ONE

Energy merging is an ability that is intrinsic to each of us. Like Jill Bolte Taylor in her experience of finding oneness while having a stroke, we all intrinsically have the potential to merge into oneness with everything at any moment.

Every human can reach oneness through the act of orgasm. But our orgasms are limited by our physiology. They depend on an act of arousal and climax and require a period of rest and recuperation, called a refractory period, before they can take place again.

**Energy merging**

Energy merging is an intentional act that, paired with the right level of development, allows us to connect to oneness. In energy merging, two or more energetic systems behave as one energetic system.

An energetic system is any being composed of

frequencies, frequency patterns, and energetic capabilities, which might or might not appear as a solid form. This can be a being with a consciousness, such as a human being, or one that doesn't have a consciousness, such as an "elements form."

## How we merge

Energy merging requires two things:
1- Energetic development
2- Knowledge of the mechanics of the energy merging practice

## Energetic development

First, energy merging requires us to achieve a certain level of energetic development. In order to merge energetically with another system, we must have the ability to vibrate like it. This refers to our vibratory knowingness. The more energies we can vibrate like, the wider and more expanded our vibratory knowingness is, and the more energetic systems we can be one with.

In energy merging, two energetic systems operate as one. They vibrate like each other. Each system maintains its own frequency patterns while adding to it the frequency patterns of the other.

During the merging process, the energetic abilities available to each system become available to both systems. When merging is repeated for a certain time, the abilities eventually become permanent in both systems.

In the example of a person seeking help from a shaman, such as the autistic child in the Horse Boy movie, the child might experience healing and transformation while the two merge for a short ceremony. But if they met regularly, for longer periods, the child would develop the abilities within himself so he can use them on himself or others without the shaman present.

Once the right level of development has been reached (which we will explore further in chapter 6), the practice is simple.

## The practice

The practice of energy merging requires the following:
- Intention
- Perception
- Focus
- Time

## Intention

Intention relates to intending to be one energetically. We have seen that some beings have consciousness while some beings don't. One of the gifts of having a consciousness is that we can intend energetically, while beings without consciousness can't.

This can be as simple as saying or thinking we intend to be one energetically with any other system. We can also use our energetic structures to intend. I mentioned earlier that a developed Sourcepoint allows us to develop the other structures. This is because we can use the Sourcepoint as a tool for intending which can enable us to merge with Source and develop these other structures.

For me, the Sourcepoint feels like an eye through which I perceive the other system before me. I intend to be one energetically with this system via the Sourcepoint.

It is important to note that we are intending a process, not a result. In energy merging, we don't intend to achieve any specific outcome. We intend to be one with whatever we face without needing things to change. We offer "our best" to the current situation, and that is enough.

## Perception

Perception is the next important element. Once I merge with this other system, I can perceive its vibratory patterns. This perception can be simply energetic, subtle and barely felt or it can overtake us like a wild tsunami of movements and sounds. It can be received through certain functions such as sensations, imagery, voices, etc.

For instance, as I sit and merge with Source, I may witness imagery or feel strong sensations in my body. This is my being perceiving the frequency patterns of Source.

Our being's energetic structures perceive the unseen energetic patterns behind everything, from an object, a symbol, a thought or other types of information. While our brain might feel the urge to jump in and translate this information into something we can understand cognitively, the practice invites us to keep our focus on the energetic frequency of the element.

## Time

Time relates to the duration of the process; the time necessary for it to be effective and complete. We continue to merge for as long as the entrainment needs to take place. We can use our intuition, previous experience, a dowsing pendulum, etc., to determine the amount of time required for the process to be completed. Often, our body, through sensations, will show us when we are done.

## Focus

There are many ways that we can focus our awareness to support the process. In terms of practice, there are 5 specific methods for energy merging. These require us to focus on our bodies, our energy bodies, and our energetic structures as part of the merging process.

## Methods for energy merging

Below are the five main methods for energy merging. The first four are from Kenneth Ray Stubbs, and the fifth is from my own experience.

1. The Sourcepoint method
2. The horizontal tube of light method
3. The diagonal tube of light method
4. The egg of white light method
5. The dissolution of form method

## 1- The Sourcepoint method

In chapter 4, we saw that the Sourcepoint is the most important energetic structure because when it is developed, it allows us to develop the other energetic structures. It is a tiny point the size of a pea located 3-4 fingers underneath the navel and halfway into the depth of the body. Once we have developed it, the Sourcepoint gives us access to the energy of all of existence.

To merge using the Sourcepoint, we engage with whatever we are merging with as if we are perceiving it through the Sourcepoint like an eye. We intend to be one energetically with whatever we are merging with using the Sourcepoint. This is our point of intention and focus.

The Sourcepoint needs to be developed for us to use it for this merging method. If it is developed but we have a hard time connecting to it or feeling it, we can instead focus on the general area around the Sourcepoint, around the lower belly area.

## 2- The horizontal tube of light method

In this method, rather than using the Sourcepoint, we visualise a horizontal tube of light extending from within our Sourcepoint into the Sourcepoint of the other being.

## 3- The diagonal tube of white light

In this method, we visualise a diagonal tube of light moving from the crown of the head, through the body within our Sourcepoint and then back into the earth beneath us. Then we visualise a similar tube of white light moving through the person we're merging with and the two tubes of white light meeting in the earth.

## 4- The egg of white light method

In this method, we visualise an egg of white light surrounding ourselves and then one surrounding the other being we intend to merge with. When the two eggs of white light begin to merge, the two energetic systems are now functioning as one. When people first begin learning energy merging, this method is often a favourite.

## 5- The dissolution of form method

In this method, we visualise an egg of white light surrounding our physical body, noticing it dissolving into tiny frequencies that merge into a field with another system.

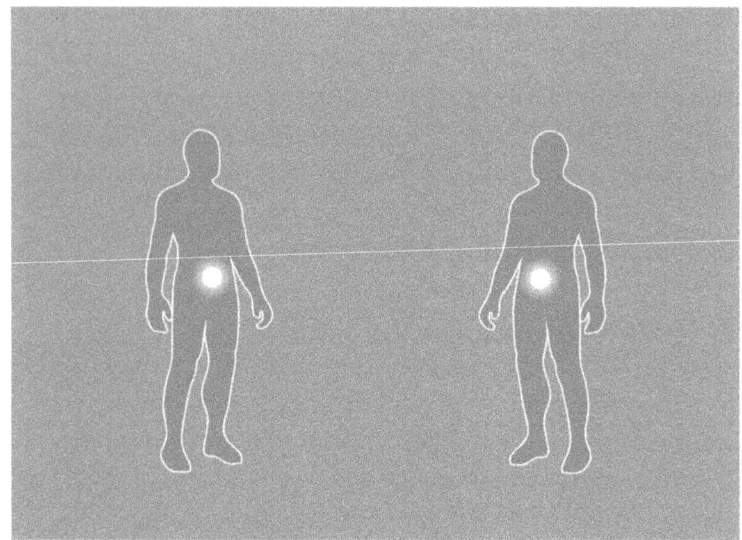

**5.1 - The Sourcepoint method**

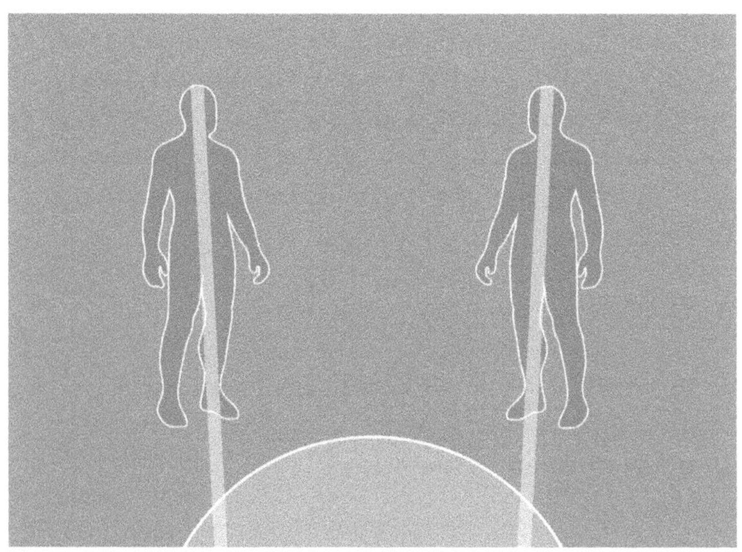

**5.3 - The diagonal tube of light method**

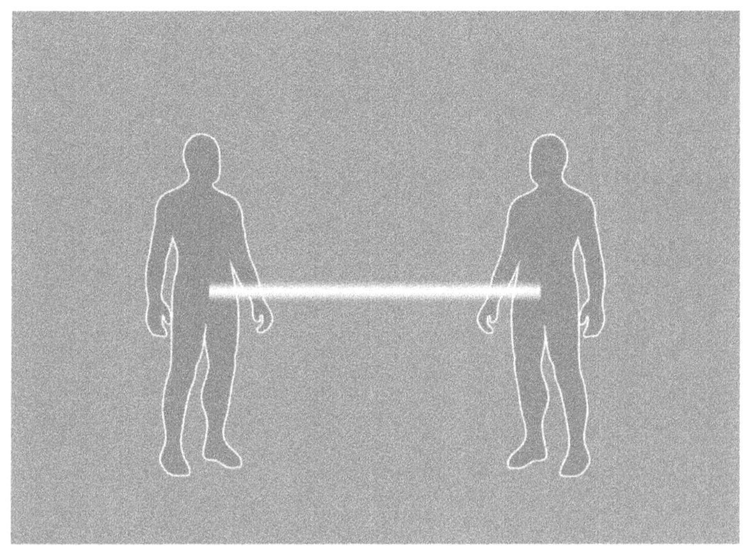

**5.2 - The horizontal tube of light method**

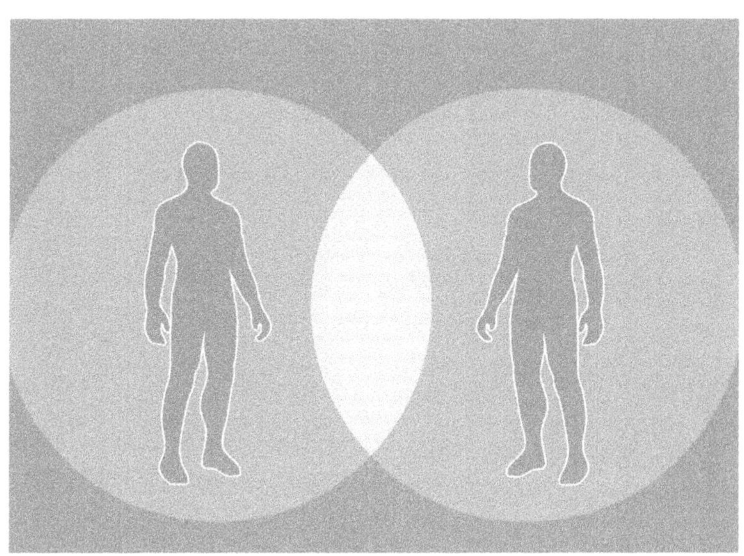

**5.4 - The egg of white light method**

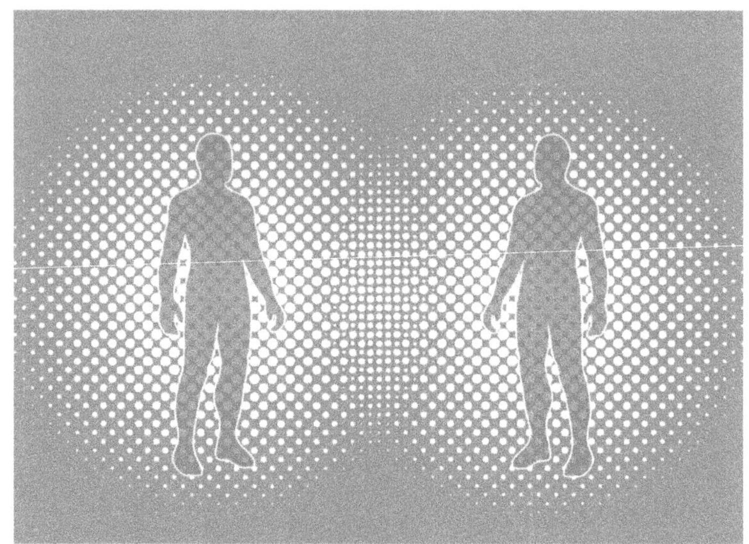

**5.5 - The dissolution of form method**

## The types of energy merging

In the following chapters, we will explore 3 main types of energy merging practices, each with a different purpose.

 1—**Merging with Source:** We can merge energetically with less-dense energies (e.g., Source) to develop our energy body.

2—**Merging with ourselves:** We can merge energetically with parts of ourselves to become more developed and whole.

3—**Merging with others:** We can merge energetically with others to support their healing and development.

**6**

# MERGING WITH SOURCE

Merging with Source is the type of energy merging that occurs during oneness experiences such as the one described in chapter 2 (when Jill Bolte Taylor had a stroke). While this type of merging can happen spontaneously, it can also be an intentional process that is highly beneficial for our development. Merging with Source allows us to develop our energy body and become an energy being.

Becoming an energy being relates to our connection to non-local, less-dense energies. As humans in form, we spend most of our lives in the world of form, which is the first plane. The more time we spend engaging with the more primordial planes, beyond the first plane, the more we develop abilities that connect us to Source. The key is to spend time in this engagement.

In his book The Physics of God, author Joseph Selbie writes about beings similar to energy beings. He refers to sages and saints who, according to religious and spiritual tales, can enable miracles. According to him, the main difference between those powerful beings and most other humans is that they know the non-local more deeply. This knowingness comes from having spent more time in direct engagement with it.

Becoming an energy being, a shaman, a sacred prostitute, or any other archetype related to these, is a developmental process with two main aspects.

1 - The development of our energetic structures
2 - The development of our vibratory knowingness

## 1- The development of our energetic structures

In chapter 3, I mentioned that we each have 20 energetic structures, some often dormant. We are generally born with 8 active energetic structures; the 12 others can be developed. To experience complete oneness, we either need to have an orgasm or have all the energetic structures developed.

## Developing the Sourcepoint

There might be many ways to develop these structures, but the one that works best for me is to connect via the Sourcepoint, the energetic intensifier that connects us to the energy of Source.

We need to develop the Sourcepoint first so we can use it to enable the connection to Source. After the Sourcepoint is developed, sustaining a continuous connection to Source supports the development of the other structures.

Developing the Sourcepoint requires us to merge energetically. Like any energy merging process, it requires intention, perception, focus, and time.

Eventually, when there is enough continuous connection, the Sourcepoint is activated.

The most efficient way of developing the Sourcepoint is with the support of a teacher who has developed the Sourcepoint themselves and actively intends to hold space for our development.

The process happens by transmission, a communication between two systems that cannot be understood by the mind but yields an impact.

For instance, my development happened while sitting in energy merging and transmission with Kenneth Ray Stubbs, as well as through numerous visits to sacred sites.

Stubbs believed his development happened when he sat with Buddhist teachers, rinpoches, and shamans. He also mentioned feeling a strong transmission from the Dalai Lama when he met him in person, a transmission so strong that he considered him one of his energetic teachers.

Ray also mentioned that he would lay out every night and look at the starry sky, intending to be one energetically with the entire universe.

He also spoke of his female lover, who, he believed, had a developed rainbow body in past incarnations. By repeatedly making love with her, an act of energetic merging, his body gained a knowingness of the rainbow body, which supported his development.

In all these cases, entrainment happens, and our being is learning to vibrate like the energy it connects to. When we stay connected, in continuous engagement, the ability to vibrate in this way becomes permanent.

The more time we spend connecting to these non-local energies, the more our energy body develops. When all the energetic structures are developed, we no longer need an orgasm to be one with everything in existence. The power of oneness becomes available to us at all times.

The rainbow body is the 21st energetic structure, and developing it signals the highest level of energetic development we can reach. All the other energetic structures must be developed before the rainbow body can be developed.

The process of developing these energetic structures is similar to that of developing the Sourcepoint. We must first be aware that these structures exist, then focus our intention on their development and continuously connect to Source.

Again, this process is greatly supported and accelerated by connecting with a field of intensified energies, with a teacher, a sacred site, etc.

## 2- The development of our vibratory knowingness

The more time we spend in direct engagement with Source, the more we are able to vibrate like more of Source, and all of existence. The ability to "vibrate like" something relates to our vibratory knowingness.

Our vibratory knowingness is our ability to "know energetically" different forms of patterns that compose our reality. When we "know" something energetically, we are vibrating like it.

The more we develop our vibratory knowingness, the more

we expand and grow, and the more resources we have access
to. Our vibratory knowingness expands as we continue
our connection to Source through the connection to the
Sourcepoint and the other energetic structures.

We are invited to engage in a practice of merging with
everything, trees, plants, stones, animals, friends, people who
challenge us, or that we simply share an elevator with. We
can merge with a beautiful meal, a sunset, or the sound of
a song being played by a violinist on the street. The more
types of patterns we merge with, the more our vibratory
knowingness increases, and our energetic body develops. As
our vibratory knowingness develops, we become able to
vibrate like (be one with) more energy patterns. Therefore we
can be one with more of life and existence.

The most beneficial way to develop our vibratory knowingess
is to merge with highly developed systems. This can include a
teacher, a shaman, a rinpoche, a sacred site, an energy power
spot, etc. In merging with them, we also get access to the
knowingness of those patterns. As they would likely already
have a very developed vibratory knowingness. Merging
with them would give us access to a wide range of frequency
patterns. Repeated exposure to those patterns allows this
knowingness to become permanent for us as well.

A being that has all the knowingness of the energetic patterns
of all beings in our universe is one that some would call
God. Eventually, we could say we are on a path of developing
the knowingness of God, who knows all of existence and
Source. No human will probably ever reach that same
knowingness, but this is our journey.

This can be a provocative concept, especially if we traditionally associate God with a more powerful, superior figure than us. Yet, we are beings of God, and this practice teaches us that the same power exists within us if we feel inclined to develop it.

## Knowing the non-local

This developmental journey takes us into the non-local realms. The more of the universe we can vibrate like, the more of the universe "we know." As we develop, we eventually vibrate like the non-local planes of existence (planes 2, 3, 4 and 5).

The more planes we can vibrate like the more developed we are and the more of life we can "be one with." According to Stubbs, when we develop our structures and our vibratory knowingness, we become able to function in these more intrinsic planes rather than simply existing in them.

The knowingness of the shaman, the one who knows, relates to a knowingness of the non-local, of Source, the 5 planes that make up the blueprint of all existence. Functioning in these more intrinsic planes allows us to support more transformation.

This is similar to what Joseph Selbie says: while every human has an expression in the non-local, the difference with a sage or miracle worker is that they can function in the non-local. By functioning there, they can effect change, and more transformation can occur. This is similar to how making a change to a house's blueprint would be much more effective than making a change to it once it is built. When we can make a change happen at the non-local level, we are making a change happen at the blueprint of existence, at the vibratory level, which will affect change in the world of form.

The ability to facilitate change in the non-local can be explained in the following way:

If a shaman can vibrate like more of existence, they can vibrate like Source. They can also vibrate like the client or whoever comes to them for support. By merging with the client, the energy being can support the client's energetic patterns to vibrate differently than they currently do (i.e. more like Source). The energy being has therefore facilitated change in the client's non-local field (energy body).

We will explore this in more detail in chapter 8.

To summarise, we need to develop all twenty energetic structures to develop energetically and become an energy being that can be one with all of existence at any time. These structures support our ability to vibrate like the more intrinsic planes and levels of density.

This development happens by spending more time connected to the field of Source and therefore knows more of existence.

I previously wrote about the great power that Jesus Christ apparently had. It would be assumed that, as the son of God, he was born quite energetically developed. However, it was also known that Jesus spent 40 days in the desert by himself, presumably cultivating this inner power.

The story of the Buddha is similar. Siddhartha Gautama, the Nepalese prince, was so moved by the world's suffering that he devoted his life to sitting under a bodhi tree. He sat under the tree for 49 days of intense meditation, observing his sensations, until he became enlightened. He became known as the Buddha and had queues of followers lining up to receive his teachings until he died.

Stubbs' energetic development was supported by various circumstances, including sitting with rinpoches and shamans, experiencing a transmission in the presence of the Dalai Lama, intending to be one with the entire universe while lying under a starry sky and repeatedly making love to a woman with an active rainbow body.

**My journey was different.**

I started by connecting with powerful land energies at sacred sites such as Stonehenge, Greek temples, the pyramids of Giza, etc., which led me to the shamanic mission in Brazil. Then, I met Stubbs and experienced his 20-level programme. Stubbs and I also created the Earth Energy project together. It was a series of ceremonies by which I would visit sacred sites, connect to Stubbs on video call, and we would merge energetically with each other, with the site, and with Source through the site. There would usually be participants, either in person or on a video call, who would join the ceremonies.

Over the years of this project, we held ceremonies at Stonehenge, Monte Alban in Mexico, the Acropolis in Athens, Kilimanjaro, the Serengeti, Sedona in Arizona and many more. Connecting at these sacred sites allowed me to develop more vibratory knowingness.

Each person's journey is unique and individual. We must first know that we have the potential to connect to Source. We then engage in direct dialogue with it, and allow it to guide us on our journey.

## Somatic shamanism

How does one actually experience this development in form? What do we feel or experience? How does it feel in the body?

The experience varies from person to person and also from moment to moment. For instance, Stubbs spoke about the time he felt a transmission in the presence of the Dalai Lama as if he had been "zapped" by him. He felt that an energy emerged and radiated from the centre of the Dalai lama's head towards the centre of his own head.

Over the years of my development, I experienced it in a variety of ways. At times, I felt nothing at all, and the mind would engage, doubting and asking "Is anything even going on?" In other moments, the body would respond with strong somatic (body-based) expressions. I would feel intense sensations and begin to sway, spiral, tremble, pulsate and undulate. Involuntary sounds would emerge and be released; I would sometimes even chant.

I realised that Source communicated with me through these expressions. It was quite helpful that, by the time I found Ray and shamanism, I had trained in somatic therapy for years and was very connected to my body's felt sense.

## Continuum movement

I mainly trained in Continuum Movement, a practice developed in California in the 60s by Emilie Conrad. It used breath, sound, movement and touch to awaken our connection to Source. Spontaneous movement would arise as a result.

The somatic practice comprises carefully crafted sequences of breath, sound, movement, and touch that allow us to connect to Source. When connected to Source, the body behaves very differently from how it does in normal everyday situations.

## The cultural anatomy vs the cosmic anatomy

Conrad referred to how we experience our bodies in everyday occurrences as the cultural anatomy. It refers to how we experience our bodies when we drive a car to the supermarket and swipe on our mobile phones. It's the modern-day "fetch wood and carry water." Our movements are linear, efficient, and often even robotic.

She refers to how we experience our bodies when connected to Source as the cosmic anatomy. This is how we are when we connect to less dense non-local energies. We move spontaneously and more fluidly. We might emit sounds different from our usual ones. In this state, we are connected to oneness, Source, and the non-local continuum.

Our body begins to experience very slow movements; our arms and legs move spontaneously and involuntarily. As some parts of our body anchor more deeply into the earth, others are suspended effortlessly in the air.

We live, breathe and exist in ways that are much more intuitive than usual. We are connected to the cosmos, and are guided by the universal system behind the creation of everything in existence.

## Movement through un-suppression

As we connect to Source through a teacher, sacred site, or another way, this energy also awakens within us. The suppression which can sometimes exist in our energy body, resulting from experiencing challenges and divisive circumstances, can be un-suppressed or released. This happens because our suppressed energy patterns are entraining to patterns which are un-suppressed (the patterns of Source).

This energetic suppression often relates to a suppression in the physical body, which can be caused by our responses to circumstances as we saw in chapter 2; through nervous system responses and the hpa axis. As less dense energies awaken in our bodies, the density stored in our physical bodies can shift as well. Movement will often arise.

There is a link between density and movement. When there is a lot of density in a physical body, movement patterns will be limited. Spontaneous movement expressions, on the contrary, can arise when density has been released. Therefore, one way this un-suppression is expressed is through spontaneous sensations, sounds, and movements that arise in the body.

These ideas are not new. Author and researcher Freddy Silva speaks of the Maya who believed that over-identification to our emotions would create patterns that would be trapped in the body. Visiting temples and sacred sites would allow these blocks to be released. The sacred site was a gateway allowing us to connect to Source. Entraining to Source energy would support the shift.

## The fluid system

According to Emilie Conrad, these spontaneous movements emerge from the body's fluid system. The fluid system includes all our biofluids: intracellular fluids such as the cytoplasm found inside our cells, nucleus and extracellular fluids, including sweat, blood, connective tissue and cerebral-spinal fluid. It comprises 66% of our body.

If our body was to be compared to the earth, the fluid system would be the earth's hydrosphere, composed of all its bodies of water: lakes, rivers, oceans, etc.

Similarly to how the hydrosphere connects every part of the earth, allowing it to function as an integrated whole, our fluid system does the same for our body, allowing it to find wholeness and integration.

The earth's hydrosphere also allows it to connect with other planets and planetary systems. Our fluid system does the same for us. It enables us to communicate with other systems, such as the less dense energies of the non-local planes.

According to continuum movement, the twisting, writhing, undulating and other spontaneous fluid movements we experience in the cosmic anatomy emerge due to the activated fluid system resulting from the somatic practice. So, while the continuum movement practice taught me how to connect to the cosmic anatomy in the body through somatic practice, shamanism and energy merging taught me I could experience a similar state through energetic development and connecting to Source.

Through shamanism, I learned this connection was a two-way street. If we can communicate with the non-local through the fluid system, the non-local must also connect with us through the fluid system.

Therefore, it made sense to me that connecting to Source would activate the fluid system, and spontaneous fluid movements would arise in our body as a response. This explained the expressions I experienced while connecting with Source through teachers and sacred sites. My body responded similarly to what I experienced in continuum movement without requiring the practice.

As our energy body connects with less dense energies, density that is stored within it can unravel. This is expressed through spontaneous movement, shaking, writhing, and spiralling, and it can also be expressed through spontaneous expressions of sound.

## Perception

Does this mean that to understand shamanism and energy merging, one must have years of training in somatic therapy? Not necessarily.

However, it is helpful to know that the body is a gateway to Source and oneness, which I learned through the practice of continuum movement. It is also important to be able to perceive the energy patterns of Source. Before we can vibrate like a specific energy pattern, we need to be able to perceive it.

This perception can happen in many ways. In my case, it happens in the body through the awareness of sensations.

**What is a sensation?**

A sensation is a physiological occurrence that arises as a result of stimuli. It is a physical feeling that results from stimulating a sense organ or sensory receptors. This includes everything from subtle ripples, pulses, twitches, gentle pressing feelings and pressure to intense aches and strong pain. The pressing in the pelvic area when we need to go to the bathroom, the pinching in the lower abdomen when we are hungry, and the raspiness in our throats when we get thirsty are all good places to start for those unfamiliar with sensations.

Unlike thoughts, they aren't understood by the mind. Unlike emotions, they do not carry stories. They are neutral; they simply "are".

**Sensations are the first order of perception.**

They are the vehicle through which we first perceive the "outside world" as embryos, foetuses and babies. Sensations are the first language we learn before verbal communication systems like English, French, or Chinese. Before we developed the cognitive ability to learn anything verbally, we had already learnt how to experience life and our surroundings through sensations.

In the face of a circumstance, such as an argument, a sunset, or a motorcycle roaring through an open road in the desert, we might feel sensations arise in our bodies. We might feel pulsations, ripples, or pressing. We can, therefore, feel anything that happens in the world around us as if it were happening within us. This includes our ability to feel Source and the entirety of the universe. This is one of the keys to oneness, therefore cultivating sensations is key. Sensations are the main way we feel our connection to Source and all of existence.

Therefore, sensations are also a way of perceiving the energetic patterns we are connecting with.

When the fluid system is awakened due to connecting to Source, for instance, sensations will often arise spontaneously. We might feel them as soft undulations, ripples, or twitches ranging from subtle to electric. Sensations are the way we feel all of existence within us.

I liken the soft ripples under my skin to those that coil across the surface of a lake or an ocean and the gentle trembling of my limbs to that of the fiery lava that pulsates within a volcano.

I liken the slight pulsations that arise so naturally in our bodies to the small green buds among the leaves of a bush that pulsate gently before opening into a rose.

These spirals, pulses and ripples are wise. They exist beyond the words and images from which we normally draw our understanding. As expressions of Source, they teach us the wisdom of the life-creating movement behind the unfolding of existence.

When we connect to Source, the sensations we feel are an embodied expression of this life-creating movement. Through sensations we see that Source exists within us. In our journey towards connecting deeper to oneness, gaining awareness of our sensations helps us better perceive the energies we have access to.

While most of my energetic development happened during the training with Stubbs and my time travelling across sacred sites, I realised the process I was experiencing would be ongoing, possibly for the rest of my life.

This process is, therefore, one of energetic merging through which a part of our being awakens, the part that is connected to Source.

I learned to see this as an eternal process of lovemaking with Source.

"A defended or rigid body not only is hampered in communicating within its own system but is removed from this depth of contact with others.

Resonance allows wholeness to be revealed bearing a mutuality of being similar to making love."

**- Emilie Conrad - Life On Land**

# 7

# MERGING WITH OURSELVES

As our energy body develops, the way we vibrate changes. We vibrate like more of existence, like non-local energies, and like Source. Since vibration affects how things come into form, a person who undergoes such a powerful energetic process will likely find their life deeply impacted by it.

This is the case for the autistic child in The Horse Boy who began to behave in more regulated ways. This is also what happened when my experience of relationships changed after the gathering with the Siberian shaman.

When two systems merge they vibrate the same way. As their vibration changes, transformation can take place. Continued exposure to this connection allows the access to this energy to become a resource that can be sustained, and eventually become more permanent.

Once this energy becomes available internally, it can be applied for transformation when needed. This is the second aspect of energy merging, the practice of bringing healing to parts of the self.

As a new connection has awakened, it gives us access to a new resource that can be applied to areas of our life where a distortion or disconnection has taken place.

Chapter 2 shared the three layers of division. While we all come from oneness, we will inevitably face circumstances that will lead us to experience disconnection and division. As a result, we will develop adaptive strategies to protect us and keep us safe. While these are beneficial, they contribute to us becoming unintegrated and less whole, and we come out of oneness.

We also saw that these adaptive strategies involve the HPA axis and nervous system responses, which leave an imprint on the physical body and create suppression in the energy body.

Energy merging allows these suppressed energies to meet the less suppressed energies of Source through transmission. Through a process of entrainment, they become less suppressed. Transformation and healing take place.

## Merging with the limited self and the unconscious

This healing process inevitably involves the exploration of the limited self and the unconscious, often referred to as the shadow. This refers to the part of our self we don't usually see and that remain in the unconscious. It includes responses to trauma, shame, and any other part of the self we feel is not worthy of love.

Most of the responses mentioned in chapter 2 will usually end up in the realm of the unconscious, simply because they tend to be challenging and we prefer to avoid exploring them.

As the relationship between the conscious and the unconscious relates to a duality, and Source is non-dual, connecting to Source inevitably leads the unconscious to come into consciousness. Hidden parts of ourselves come to light and are given space to be seen and processed. We find ourselves required to face old shadows we might usually avoid.

This is similar to what the Maya experienced when visiting temples and unravelling emotional blocks that were held in the body. As they connected to the temples and accessed less polarised energies, the polarised emotional patterns in their bodies unravelled.

While all these distortions exist in our body as density, they also exist energetically. Any emotional block or issue becomes reflected as energetic suppression. Merging with the more suppressed parts of the self allows us to bring the resource of oneness and Source to this suppression. A process of energetic un-suppression takes place because the suppressed energy is entrained with an energy that is less suppressed. As a result, our limitations can be expanded and we can become more whole.

As these limitations unravel, our unconscious comes into consciousness. We might receive images or insights linked to parts of ourselves we don't usually see as these come into the light to be resolved.

This process happens through the same energy merging process we have seen until now, which involves (1) intention, (2) perception, (3) focus and (4) time:

1- **Intention:** We intend to be one energetically with this part of us that feels disconnected.
2- **Perception:** We perceive its patterns within our system.
3- **Focus:** We focus on these using the Sourcepoint or another method
4- **Time:** We focus in this way for a specific amount of time

until the process is complete.

Perception is key. Perceiving the disconnection makes it possible to merge with it. This is where the ability to perceive sensations comes in handy. If we can experience this disconnection as sensations in the body, such as pulsations, twitches, pressing, etc., we can focus on these and become one with them. The division can dissolve, and we can become more integrated.

This type of energy merging is related to the process of merging with Source from chapter 6. As we merge energetically with the less-dense energies of Source, the parts of the self that are affected by division, which are more suppressed and dense energies, arise and want to be seen.

In my years travelling to sacred sites and enabling ceremonies, which connected me to Source, I've had no choice but to walk through fire and face my demons. On numerous occasions, I have found myself almost paralysed when facing moments of darkness and contraction. The more I committed to this work, the more darkness arose.

I also experienced incredible expansion and clear presence as my whole body vibrated from a sense of oneness and flow.

We can experience all of it in the body. We experience the cosmic whispers that express themselves through sensations, ripples and micro-movements arising within us.

This is a process of reconciliation between the part of the self which is intrinsically connected to Source and the part which has experienced division as a result of facing circumstance.

## Somatic therapy

In a way, this is a form of somatic therapy. Somatic therapy is a healing process that uses the felt sense of the body (i.e. sensations) to support the healing of trauma, stress and unresolved emotional issues.

Somatic refers to the soma, which is our body. More specifically, it is the living body, an inhabited body that can feel itself and all life in sensations.

For instance, a sunset, a sunrise, an emotional block, or a disagreement with a family member can all be perceived as sensations within the body. When we can feel everything in our sensations, we know we have everything within us. We can therefore begin to be one with it.

When we can be one with something, we are no longer in division with it, and our relationship to it can change. It can be experienced neutrally, come into oneness and can begin to change.

Most importantly, as we can feel anything in our body, we can also feel Source in our body. The energy of Source becomes a resource available to us at any moment, which can be applied, integrated and merged into aspects of our life that seek to fall into balance.

## Beyond words

Our energy body exists at a deeper, more intrinsic level than the layer of psychology, where our emotions and nervous system responses exist. It is also below the level of conscious thinking that is limited by our perspectives. Working energetically therefore allows us to work more intrinsically and non-locally, at the root of the disconnection.

Much of our trauma is initiated in the stages of our development which are pre-verbal. This can be referred to as implicit developmental trauma that takes form at a stage of development before our cognition is developed enough to understand anything. While this type of trauma can be addressed with talk therapy, healing modalities that are pre-verbal, non-local and more intrinsic can often be more beneficial.

## Integrating the totality of everything

In these spaces of stillness, we truly see ourselves. We experience a process of internal lovemaking in which every part of the self is merged together and integrated. Contractions meet expansions; our shadows' pains, challenges and distortions meet the pleasure, power and gifts of our inner medicine.

We can witness the shadows of our trauma and shame alongside waves of extreme bliss and power. We can hold all of it. We can also connect to the neutral space that is beyond them.

What would the full pain of our darkest shadow look like if we didn't have to censor it like we normally do in everyday situations? Would it appear as a storm of flaming demons spewing out familiar words of self-criticism?

What would happen if we merged with this energy rather than suppressed it? What alchemy can occur when this density is given room to breathe, expand, erupt and finally find rest?

This process invites us to expand beyond our usual ideas, in which we might perceive contractions as something bad that should be avoided or suppressed. Both contractions and expansions are needed for our universe to survive. If it were to only expand, the universe would explode. If it were to only contract, it would implode. The dance between expansion and contraction allows our system to stay in balance.

For us to reach oneness, we must merge with all of it; with the pain of our contractions and the pleasure of our expansions. Oneness, by definition, includes all of it, with no exception. Merging with these dense energetic patterns also allows us to expand our vibratory knowingness and become more whole.

The process of sitting with the darkness, shadows and limitations is supported by the access to resources that become available as we merge with Source. We can engage with something that feels extremely dark while knowing we are simultaneously connected to Source. We can face demons and limitations more easily when we know we have access to a greater power.

Through communion with darkness, we also find truth. We realise that oneness doesn't only exist in the delicious sensual ripples and ecstatic waves of pleasure that run through our bodies in orgasm but also in the density, contractions and tensions that appear to challenge us.

## The window of tolerance

As we sit with these uncomfortable sensations, our vibratory knowingness develops and we gain the ability to be one with more of life and existence. In the realm of somatic therapy and trauma, this relates to the concept of the window of tolerance.

The window of tolerance is the range of emotions and stress levels a person can experience while remaining balanced and regulated. When we are within this window, we can handle circumstances without feeling activated, overwhelmed or shutting down.

When a person is affected by trauma or has experienced consistent stressors, as we have seen in chapter 2, the window of tolerance can get smaller. As a result, the range of circumstances we are able to cope with is smaller and we react more intensely to stressors. We might become too anxious and overwhelmed or feel numb and disconnected.

Being above the window of tolerance refers to hyper-arousal. We feel panicked, anxious, or overwhelmed, perhaps experiencing a "fight or flight" mode. These responses relate to the sympathetic branch of the autonomic nervous system.

Being below the window of tolerance refers to hypo-arousal. We might feel numb, disconnected, or emotionally shut down. These responses are related to the parasympathetic branch of the autonomic nervous system.

Experiencing trauma or being repeatedly exposed to stressors can create links between certain stimuli and specific stress responses (such as activation or shutting down.) These responses can sometimes be hijacked and used in ways that are out of proportion with the stimulus. This is illustrated in chapter 2 by the example of the sophisticated alarm system that intends to keep a house safe from robbery, yet gets set off by a butterfly.

Our window of tolerance becomes more narrow, and as a result, the range of circumstances we are able to "be with" is reduced.

Somatic therapy teaches us how this process affects the body. When we experience uncomfortable circumstances, we tend to experience sensations we would rather avoid. We will, therefore, use coping mechanisms to numb and escape these. This inability to be with our sensations narrows our tolerance window.

As we merge with more of life by merging with parts of ourselves (as per this stage of the merging process) we find ourselves able to be one with sensations that would otherwise be uncomfortable and that we would normally avoid.

Our vibratory knowingness increases and our window of tolerance can expand.

We can be one with more of life and existence.

"Know thyself,
 and you shall know
 the universe and God."

- Quote from the temple of Apollo at Delphi.

**8**

# MERGING WITH OTHERS

What differentiates the energy being from most other "normal folk" is their commitment to their practice. As we have seen, the practice involves connecting to the power of Source and applying it to the aspects of their lives that need healing. After enough time continuously engaging in this way, they can support others with a similar process.

As they become bridges to Source for themselves, they become bridges to Source for others, too. Through the force of entrainment, the same access to power that awakens within them awakens within whoever they connect with.

The energy being has also sat with so much of their own darkness that they can help others sit with theirs.

When they can hold enough of themselves in love and oneness, they can help others hold themselves in love and oneness, too. They teach by transmission, saying very little or no words.

**The energy being**

Like the shaman, the energy being is also "the one who knows." This is not a knowingness of wisdom but rather a knowingness of the non-local Source.

It is, in fact, a vibratory knowingness developed by spending continuous amounts of time merging with as much of existence as possible: high-intensity beings, lands, unconscious shadows, Source, etc.

This aligns perfectly with what scientist and author Joseph Selbie writes in The Physics of God. The main difference between most humans and those we consider sages and saints is that they know the non-local more deeply, mainly because they have spent more time directly engaging with it.

Spending time in this direct engagement allows us to vibrate like the energy of the non-local and affect change there. As the non-local contains the blueprint behind everything, engaging with something non-locally will inevitably bring about a change in the local world of form, usually more easily.

The energy being generally has developed more abilities and energetic structures and access to more resources than most humans. Merging energetically with them is beneficial, as it allows others to gain access to these same resources.

This does not make them superior beings. The energy being is not trying to play God or to be a healer.

They could be likened to someone with a PhD in physics or pharmaceutical studies who can support the healing of others not because they are superior but because they invested the time required to achieve a knowingness.

Their role is to transmit; to bring presence, intentionality, focus, and commitment to any situation. They merge with it as one and share resources with it. This is done without a specific intention. We don't intend to heal anyone but rather to share our resources. If these can be used, they will.

This level of development allows them to teach by transmission, often without saying or doing anything.

**How do we teach by transmission?**

An energy being can teach by transmission first because they have developed the capacity to vibrate like energy patterns other than their own. The more they develop and grow through practice, the more they gain a knowingness of Source. As a result, they are able to merge with more of existence. This allows them to merge with people, clients, patients, lovers, etc. It also allows them to merge with other forms, such as a piece of land, a circumstance, a health issue, a pain or other distortion.

Therefore, they have the ability to facilitate others simply by merging with them with focused intention. The energy being intends to be one with the other energetic system. The "teaching" happens as the two beings entrain and vibrate similarly. In that space of merging, the power available to the energy being awakens within the other person (we might call a client). This power becomes available to the client and can be used to support the client's healing or transformation.

When the two systems become one, the energy being can perceive the patterns of the other being. They can perceive whatever is happening within them, including any disconnection that is seeking attention. They might experience this perception through an awareness of sensations, voices, colours, and imagery. Most often, they will feel these patterns as sensations in their own soma (body), allowing them to bring awareness to them.

They can then process whatever they perceive in their own soma the same way they process their healing in their personal practice: by merging with it.

By force of entrainment, the healing process that occurs within the energy being's system also becomes available to the other system, the client. The latter might not be fully aware of the mechanics of the process, but they will often feel something is going on.

In that moment, the two are in a space of shared resources. The access to Source available to the energy being is available to the client while they merge. They simply need to be present with the process and stay attentive to it and to each other. The client doesn't need to be as energetically sensitive as the energy being. However, it is much more beneficial if they are also attuned to the subtle, energetic process.

Eventually, as people spend more time in this connection, the access to this energy becomes permanent, and they can facilitate themselves on their own. Eventually, they can also facilitate others. While it may not be in everyone's life path to become an energy being, the ability to develop in this way and impact the lives of others with the power of our presence is available to all of us.

**What does the process look like?**

In contrast to the intricate shamanic ceremonies we expect to witness, the energy merging process can appear quite subtle. The energy being and client might just sit still with each other, and to the outsider, it might appear that nothing is happening at all.

As the energy being connects to Source, they might experience some expressions similar to those I shared in chapter 6, which relate to the cosmic anatomy. They might shake, writhe, make spontaneous sounds.

The client might experience their own version of the cosmic anatomy as well. I have seen clients shake, writhe, cry, and even orgasm simply by sitting together and merging.

I will share more about my experience as a facilitator in chapter 9.

Sometimes, it can also feel like nothing is happening, and doubt can arise. Sometimes, the session is subtle, but the impact is felt days or weeks later. We are required to trust the process and the unseen hands that are at work.

**The process doesn't always "work."**

Sometimes, it might seem the process didn't "work". People might wish for a certain impact, but a different one will occur.

Our job is to sit with the circumstances or inquiry, to merge with it, thus sharing our greatest resources with it. We do not intend any specific outcome. What is meant to happen will happen and sometimes the outcome is not what we wish.

Perhaps the autistic child will not see their symptoms diminished, or the financial issues will not be resolved. Like with any facilitator-client relationship, it is also possible the two are simply not a match or that the practice was not a match for the client.

However, it is also possible that the outcome we hoped for was not aligned with the truth. We are invited to simply be open and experience the truth meant to arise for us.

## Everything is as it should be

The connection to Source connects us to the universal force behind the creation of everything. It is the force that powers a tornado, opens the petals of a flower, turns a sperm and egg into a cell, and turns an embryo into a human being. The force turns a seed into a small bush or tree that can then drop lemons to the earth with a soft, "local" thump.

Connecting to this force allows us to experience the universe's effortless flow. As a result, it helps us see that everything is exactly as it should be.

In fact, this is the main impact I have experienced most consistently through the practice of energy merging over the years: the ability to see that things are exactly as they should be and nothing needs to change.

This allows us to see the gift in any situation rather than focus on wanting to change it. This already can enable transformation as a shift in perspective can often be all that is needed. Remember that our consciousness and expectations affect the way things vibrate; therefore, they affect the way they come into form.

The ability to see the gift in everything results from entraining to the energy of Source. As I wrote in chapter 2, Source has no problems. Source knows that everything is as it should be, whether it may appear so on the surface or not.

## The "failed" jewellery shop: a case study

I remember one situation at the beginning of my time as an energy being: I worked with a client who owned a small jewellery shop in Barcelona. The shop was in a difficult financial state, and the client feared she might have to close it down. It barely made one sale daily, which was not enough to survive.

In a session with this client, I merged energetically with her and the situation. It was clear that the client wanted the shop to turn around and be financially successful. I intended to be one with her and the situation, but I had no other goal or objective.

A few days after the process ended, she called me, frantic, telling me the situation had worsened. Since our session, even the one daily sale she usually made had disappeared and the shop was on track to close.

While she was furious and panicked, I felt calm. I had every certainty that things were exactly as they should be.

I hadn't heard from this woman for a while, but one day, I walked by the shop and saw it had closed.

Months later, she rang me and invited me for a glass of wine. I was surprised to hear from her and accepted the invitation, although I was unsure what to expect.

When I met her at the bar, she smiled from ear to ear. She said she had invited me to a glass of wine to thank me. After our process, the shop closed down, and she went through a dark time at first. Within weeks, a man showed up out of the blue and offered her an ideal job.

She had moved to a small island and was enjoying life on the beach, supported by a job she loved and ideal conditions. Life was abundant, and she no longer had to deal with the stress of trying to make a failing shop work.

I believe that, as we merged, the situation aligned with Source and truth. The store's closing was precipitated, allowing for the perfect job situation to arise. Most importantly, she had the clarity to see that everything, despite appearing as a catastrophe, was exactly as it should be.

The ability to see that everything is as it should be relates to the level of suppression in our energy body. The defense structures that result from past experiences keep us looking for what is wrong in everyday situations rather than seeing what is right with them.

As these patterns get unsuppressed, our defense structures can also shift and loosen. We no longer see life under the filtered lens of our protective mechanisms. Instead, we can see life in a more clear and unfiltered way.

## The dismantling of illusions

While travelling in Yucatan, I met a Mayan woman who told me some of the stories of her ancestors. They believed life was as illusionary as a virtual reality game.

She and her brothers and sisters would be left alone in a dark cave at a young age to be with their thoughts and could only leave the cave when they realised none of them were real. What they perceived as "life" was only a virtual reality game.

I have experienced this dismantling of illusion with the practice of energy merging. The illusionary contracts we have been bound too collapse, and we see life for the truth that it is.

Everything is exactly as it should be.

Anything else is an illusionary part of the delusion of divisiveness.

**Is everything really as it should be?**

This can be a radical thought.

Oftentimes, when I speak this, people will reply with statements such as, "How about a situation in which thousands of children are being killed in a war or a genocide? Is that meant to be?"

Indeed, this is where it becomes a radical thought. I sense that major, disastrous catastrophes are usually meant to show us where we have forgotten love. I dare to hope that the death of thousands of children or other tragic circumstances, serve our collective to move more fully and deeply towards love. Whether we accept this invitation or not is up to us. Would it be better if we could learn love in other ways that didn't involve such tragedies? Absolutely. But the flow serves us the medicine in just the way we are ready to receive it in the precise moment.

Those who see the god in themselves
allow others to see the god in themselves, too.
There is no greater way to transform the world.

## Common facilitation Q&A's

Some questions or concerns sometimes arise when discussing energy merging as a healing practice for supporting others.

### Q: How do I protect myself and my energy?

This is a common question among energy workers who may have learned other practices, such as Reiki. As someone attuned as a Reiki master, I remember a strong emphasis on protection and clearing energies that "aren't ours."

An empathetic energy healer often takes on another person's energy patterns, which replace some of their own. This can feel invasive and overwhelming.

The process of energy merging is different.

In energy merging, when an energy being perceives the client's energy patterns, they maintain all their own energy patterns and resources; nothing is replaced.

Rather than wanting to push away or heal something that we would normally refer to as "bad energy" or "low-frequency" energy, the energy being instead brings it into awareness and merges with it. By doing so, they offer it resources, such as those available through the connection to Source. The relationship to this energy can therefore change.

I also hear concerns relating to what is considered energetic "draining." People who generally identify as empaths often become concerned that they feel drained when they connect energetically with others, as if others are "sucking" their energy. In these cases, they usually resort to energetic protection and shielding methods to keep their field clear of draining or "negative" energies.

The more energetically developed we become, the more capable we are of remaining grounded in our own frequency and supporting the transmutation of other energies we engage with. We can find a new way of relating with energies we normally refer to as "negative" or "low frequency."

Methods of energetic protection become less necessary when we develop more abilities.

**Q: Am I taking on an energy that is not mine?**

When discussing energy work, practitioners often refer to "what is mine vs. what is not." They often say they prefer to return to clients what "is theirs" at the end of the session to protect themselves. Considering the mechanics of this process, protection and clearing are not necessary. In fact, protection feels contradictory to a model rooted in oneness. A model in which some energies are positive, some negative, some good, some bad, or high or low frequency is polarised and distances us from oneness.

In many ways, this work is about reminding people that every part of them is worthy of love. If we were to hand them back what "is theirs" and say, "This is not mine!" it might not be supportive of a process meant to support them feeling loved.

The truest power of this work lies in oneness. Oneness is not exclusionary. It inevitably includes everything. Energy merging requires us to look at everything from a neutral perspective rather than a lens of polarity. We can merge with something seen as potentially damaging when we know we are resourceful enough to be able to hold it.

In the realm of oneness, the idea that "this is mine, or this is yours" is irrelevant. Rather, "It's here; it's what it is; let's be one with it."

This idea also relates to our ability to trust the flow of life. If something comes to an energy being via a client, a workshop participant, or any other way, we must know it is coming for a reason; it is not random. It often comes to show us something that exists within ourselves that we would benefit from seeing and processing.

I see these dense energies as a reflection of the parts of our own being that are still dense and ready to be transmuted. Being in touch with these energies is an invitation to develop ourselves energetically in new ways.

A good example of this is the story of the Hawaiian practice of Ho'oponopono and its creator, Dr. Len. Dr. Len famously supported the healing of an entire hospital ward of mentally ill criminals without meeting any of them personally. He sat in the ward, read their files, and acknowledged their pains and disruptions. He then looked inward and recognised that everything that existed within those patients existed within him, too. Over time, as these would heal within him, the patients were cured and released from the ward one by one.

Certainly, seeing all the flaws of the world within us can be heavy and daunting. It's important to have a foundational sense of the resources within us to support the healing process.

It may seem overwhelming to believe we are meant to merge with everything. The energy being can have their boundaries.

We can always say no to a client and not merge with something.

When an energy being faces something that feels too much, they can also see it as an invitation to stretch their energetic capacities, and expand their window of tolerance. They can do so by increasing their access to resources, such as the energy of Source.

While people are often surprised to hear about this model and will sometimes resist it at first, they usually find it a much more resourceful way of doing energy work.

For many people, including myself, energy merging leaves them much less depleted than the act or intention of "giving" or "sending" energy. The fact that this work invites us to share energy with others from a resourced place, where we have filled our cup first, is more sustainable and supportive for the practitioner.

**Q: If we can entrain and vibrate like less dense energies (such as Source), can we also entrain to dense energies? Such as energy we would characterise as bad or even dangerous?**

When two energy systems merge and become one, we entrain to the energy that is less dense. This is because our natural inclination, as energetic systems, is to naturally move towards the less dense energies.

In science, this can be supported by exploring the concept of entropy.

Entropy is the process by which our entire universe is created. It is a measurement of disorder and density.

Low entropy relates to lower disorder, which means higher order. Higher order manifests as higher density.

High entropy relates to higher disorder. Higher disorder relates to lower density.

Therefore:

Low entropy = higher density
High entropy = lower density

Entropy is a process of slow decline into disorder and randomness by which particles naturally move from being denser to less dense. A great way to visualise it is by picturing a glass bottle smashing into pieces.

For instance, if a car wheel is punctured, the air inside it will leave the wheel rather than the air outside it entering the hole and filling it.

Everything always naturally moves from more dense to less dense. This leads us to our eventual dissolution and death. Therefore, it makes sense that if a certain energetic system merges with another one, the two will entrain to energies that are less local and dense, as this is our natural inclination. It is the movement of the entire universe.

**Q: What about cases in which a person is possessed by an entity or evil spirit? Is this a merging of two energies as well? Is this not one energetic system entraining to a more dense energy?**

No. When two energy systems merge, they keep their own energetic patterns and the other system's patterns are added to those patterns. The system expands energetically. In a case in which a person has been possessed by an entity or another spirit, there is not an expansion but rather a contraction.

A person is normally possessed by an entity or spirit when that spirit is looking for a body to inhabit. They usually do so when they feel they need to complete a process they did not have the time to complete while still alive in human form. For instance, if a person feels they died too soon, they still want to see their child or engage in a romance with an ex-lover, they will seek a human being that they can take over. For a human being to be taken over, they generally tend to have a weak sense of self and be less integrated or whole.

For instance, a person who is whole, as a result of continuously connecting to Source, will be less likely to be overtaken by a spirit or entity.

This is why our work as energy beings is to strengthen our connection to Source. As we connect to Source more, we become more whole and develop a stronger sense of self.

Exorcism is, therefore, not a process of removing an energy from someone but rather one of supporting healing for two people, the person who has been taken over and the one who is taking them over. Both need resolution.

**Q: Is it unethical/invasive to merge with a person when they aren't aware it's happening?**

When we hold space for a client, we assume their consent to merge energetically with them as this is generally what they will come to us for.

If we merge with others as part of a process of personal growth or to heal parts of ourselves, they might not be aware we are doing it and may not have explicitly consented to it. It's thus a good idea to question if this is unethical. Are we invading a person's energetic field in an intrusive way?

In the practice of energy merging, we are not sending energy to others, nor are we entering their field. We are making our resources available to them and offering them the possibility of sharing them with us. This sharing allows them to awaken similar resources that exist within them, if they feel called to it.

They might feel this access and use the resources if they wish. If they don't, nothing will happen. This is why it's more beneficial for the person to be aware of what is happening or at least stay focused on us.

**The shaman's breath**

The shaman's breath in the morning light
Glides on the skins, undressing shames,
Entering lungs and leaves with shadows.

The shaman's breath in the morning light
Cleanses their dreams, making them wild.
You feel me inside, at your core beneath the earth.

The shaman's breath in the morning light
They are panting with animals; hands, grunts and blood.
You kiss my tears, swallow my smile.

Unbinding our ropes, united as one,
We burnt ourselves and exhaled in unison
The shaman's breath in the morning light.


- Julien Finlay

**9**

# BECOMING AN ENERGY BEING

My journey as a case study

My journey as an energy being started on a Greek Island in 2010. I was 30, a successful interior designer based in London and Paris. A holiday in Mykonos with my partner would kick off a series of unexpected circumstances that would change my life.

For years, my partner and I had been entertaining a Parisian romance that had been fiery and dramatic from the start. Imagine CDs being catapulted through the air, belongings dramatically thrown from windows, and shouting matches which would regularly shake the solid foundations of our home's Haussmannian structure.

Despite that, neither of us was ready for what happened one night in Mykonos.

We had a fight; one that was the climax of a wave of tension that began in a nightclub a few nights before. I became infuriated by an off-the-cuff remark he made which alluded to him finding someone else more attractive than me.

It was silly, I know. I should have been able to let it go, but I couldn't. I had experienced rejection and pain for my physical appearance for as long as I could remember and was plagued with insecurities. As a child of immigrant parents who was overweight and considered unattractive, I continuously felt rejected by the peers I wanted to be accepted by.

Hearing that comment, in the nightclub in Mykonos, led me to feel like an insecure prom queen catching her boyfriend stare at another girl's blouse. I felt enraged. My reaction, though petty and foolish, was entirely beyond my control. The shadows which had haunted me for the first thirty years of my life were screaming loudly and had deafened me to the voice of reason.

The years of rejection by the schoolmates I longed to be accepted by led to the creation of a "story" of constant rejection that felt violent and lasted decades. I became hyper-vigilant and trained myself to see threats everywhere, even when they didn't exist.

As these feelings remained unaddressed and unprocessed, they cultivated a savage underworld of insecurity that underscored everything.  Moments in which a partner might find someone else more attractive would, therefore, trigger a deep fear of loss and a need for survival. Rational thinking couldn't survive in the swamp.

By the time I met Henri, my hyper-vigilance had peaked. Everything needed to be perfect, and so did I. As a successful interior designer, I spent my days designing millionaire homes, upmarket London hotels and fashion shops for the most picky fashion designers.

I planned my days around obsessive workouts and perfectly controlled meals. I yearned to be physically flawless and to become the "ideal gay man". The muscular, socially accepted body I was creating became the metaphorical "protective shell" I needed to survive. All of it had led up to that chaotic yet pivotal moment.

So, we had a fight. It involved stomachs being kicked, jaws being punched, and furniture being dragged as our bodies were flung across the room.

It was partially caused by my inability to dismiss Henri's insignificant comments, and partially by his inability to manage his work pressures and persistent drug and alcohol problem.

I remember the taste of cocaine as I kissed his lips. My blood boiled, and my temperature rose. He pushed back and challenged me.

I remember thumping my fist into the bed and screaming, "NON!" without knowing what I was saying no to.

I don't remember who took the first hit. It doesn't matter. Our bodies grappled violently for I-don't-know-how-long. It felt like hours, years, decades.

The force of our savage exchange moved furniture across the room, thumping the walls and scratching the floors.

Like untamed jungle animals trapped in a small cave, we fought until we reached exhaustion, then collapsed on the two twin beds pulled apart in the storm.

I had never experienced physical violence in a relationship, so the event rattled me. We instantly parted ways, agreeing to meet on the beach a few days later when the dust would settle to discuss the future of our relationship.

Our conversation was brief. I was unable to meet his desire for us to bury our heads in the sand and forget the events that had taken place. As no resolution could be reached, we decided to break up.

I stood up from the sun lounger and walked away. I walked about fifty meters when I was stopped dead in my tracks. An intense sensation in my legs turned into numbness, and they soon could no longer move.

My arms then joined them and soon, my entire body was paralysed. My heart thumped ferociously, expanding and overtaking me.

My vision blurred, and I noticed the outlines of my body softening, slowly dissolving.

My arms, legs, hips and feet began to melt into their surroundings. Like my body, the outlines of the environment also began to blur. The sand, the sea, the sky, the tiny white houses, and the burned trees scattered on the barren hills all started to melt into one large spiral that merged with my physical body.

It was unlike anything I had ever experienced. I was somehow becoming one with the world around me, and all I could do was let go.

Shades of purple, pink and orange appeared out of nowhere. It was surreal and otherworldly, as a good psychedelic trip would be. What I previously thought of as my body was now an amalgamation of waves and spirals, merging into a blurry,

multicoloured hologram.
I was no longer apart from everything else in existence.
I was at one with it all. The earth, the stars, the universe and the pulse of God. I found euphoria, ecstasy and bliss in this cosmic embrace.

At that moment, the usual concepts of time, place and identity disappeared. I felt I was suspended in the infinite now, between the events of the past and of those yet to come.

I couldn't tell you how long this lasted. I only remember suddenly feeling my body return to its usual solid form. My heart was pounding, my arms and legs trembling, and tears cascading down my cheeks. I felt like I had been freed from a full-body cast that had confined me for a long time.

Once again, the sea was to my left, the sky high above my head and the earth under my feet, where it had always been.

My eyes squinted, adjusting to the brightness of the sun. My lips, mouth and tongue stretched into a strange grimace as if I was trying to break a mask. My hands floated up to my cheeks as I rediscovered the physicality of my face. Fortunately, or unfortunately, I was human again, whatever that meant…

In that short moment, I released my relationship with Henri, my life in Paris and possibly even some of my attachment to a lifetime of unregulated torment.

When I returned home, everything changed. Until then, my spiritual life had been limited to attending a handful of meditation circles in central London and flipping through the pages of a Dalai Lama book. The idea of having a oneness experience was foreign to me. I turned to Tantra to attempt

to make sense of the event which had taken place.
I enrolled in a one-year tantra training, where I discovered somatic therapy and the continuum movement practice.

I began to experience the cosmic anatomy, the Source of life expressing itself within my body through spontaneous movements, waves, undulations, ripples, and twitches.

My body would shake and writhe uncontrollably in ways that were new to me. These somatic experiences were deeply nourishing and informative, allowing me to experience parts of myself that were previously unexplored. I received insights that, for once, did not come from the mind but from the body. These felt purer and more truthful than the thoughts that usually ran my daily life.

Focusing on these spontaneous expressions of the body for long periods which  led me to altered states of awareness, which even caused me to experience hallucinations at times. The images that appeared felt real and vivid and were initially disturbing. After a while, I realised they showed me what was lurking in the shadows. Some seemed related to current events, others to the past, and some felt completely distant, as if coming from previous incarnations.

I saw a prisoner huddled and locked in a dark solitary confinement cell in India.

I saw a Malaysian girl, perhaps ten or eleven years old, who appeared to have been sold into sex slavery.

These memories, which spanned decades and lifetimes, all felt like they were happening in this precise, infinite moment. The continuum of the now.

After a few years of being immersed in these somatic practices, another cornerstone experience occurred after visiting the famous temple of Wat Arun, a sacred site in Bangkok. I was visiting a museum gift shop when I began to experience uncontrollable spasms in my arms and legs. I rushed to my hotel to give the experience space.

On arrival, my body began to shake even more wildly and uncontrollably. I tore off my clothes and leapt into bed. My body began to shake violently, and reptilian movements emerged, running across my midline and spine.

Soon, chants emerged from my throat with a power so remarkable they even aggressively jolted my head left to right as if it were being pulled by an aggressor.

For hours, I let the chants move me, and I dropped in and out of various altered states of awareness, similar to those I assume one might experience on psychedelics. At some point, it all became so big and overpowering that I even feared this new state would become my new default. I worried I had become a crawling snake-like being, only sliding and writhing rather than standing and walking. For the rest of my life, I would be condemned to chant words unrecognisable to most humans rather than everyday speech.

I continued to move in and out of altered states before finally passing out. It must have been hours later when my phone rang and woke me up. I felt shaken and vulnerable as if a thick layer of my being had been ripped away, exposing the vulnerability of a newborn child.

It was hard for me to make sense of what happened that day,

so I reached out for help.

A friend later told me I had spoken the language of God. I understood that visiting the temple had exposed me to an energetic transmission that significantly impacted me.

The experience led me to leave my life as a London designer, move to Barcelona, and start a new, unknown path.

Only weeks after arriving in Barcelona, Honi told me at the end of the sunrise ceremony that I was a shaman. At the time, I didn't know what a shaman was. When I asked her what to do next, she answered, "Nothing. Just wait."

Less than 24 hours later, I received a phone call from a woman I didn't know, inviting me to Mongolia to design a building for the Ministry of Arts and Culture in Ulaanbataar.

"We leave in 2 weeks. Are you in?"

I said yes without truly knowing what I was saying yes to.

After a quick online search, I discovered that Mongolia had been a hotspot for shamanism, which was previously its main religion until Buddhism overtook it in the 17th century.

On arrival at Ulanbataar, we discovered that the building we were meant to re-design was being squatted by a family, and the project was paused indefinitely.

Having been gifted some free time, I began a hunt for a shaman that seemed to lead nowhere.

Eventually, while on my way to a Buddhist monastery, a

couple of large totem poles caught my eye. I followed my intuition and was led down a mysterious path to a shaman's yurt with big golden doors. Upon entering, I was struck by a collection of taxidermy animals, cups full of blood, and a cage full of rabbits probably waiting to be sacrificed.

I had a short exchange with a hostile shaman before leaving the yurt confused. Instead of bringing me closer to the shamanic initiation I was hoping for, I felt even more distanced and disconnected from it.

I continued my Mongolia trip, visiting a tribe of Yak herders on barren fields 22 hours away from the city. An online search yielded a 200-page academic guide on Mongolian shamanism, which included instructions on how to carry out a shamanic ceremony. I asked the family of yak herders if they would be open to me conducting a ceremony for them. They agreed.

They organised a fire, which was required for the ceremony; I gathered the stones and feathers I needed and spent the afternoon practising my drumming and chanting. Finally, the night came, and we gathered around the fire. The fire was roaring, the stones were in place, and I began chanting and drumming with feathers around my neck.

The chants evolved into spontaneous sounds similar to the ones I experienced in Thailand. I lost myself in a moment beyond time and place. It wasn't as intense as the dissolving I felt in Mykonos, but I knew I was reaching an altered state.

Eventually, I returned to the "here and now" and realised that the sound had stopped and the ceremony was ending. The family cheered, applauded and thanked me, and we got up from the fire to go to bed.

The night was filled with a series of strange visions kept me awake. There were clear flashes of people I didn't know who seemed to be speaking to me. They would come, go and come back, and it made little sense.

Eventually, I found myself even seeing imagery with my eyes open. It seemed like a light show at first, but eventually, it began to look like a female figure moving through the yurt towards me.

I could feel her getting closer and closer. I froze with my eyes open and stared at her until she disappeared. I blinked my eyes a few times and realised she, whoever she was, was gone, and everything was back to normal.

When I awoke at sunrise, I decided to dialogue with the sky, the land, and the entire universe. I knew a big shift was coming, and I found myself speaking confidently to what seemed to be a greater power beyond me.

"Whatever it is, I am ready for it."

A voice arose from within as if the land were speaking through my body. It told me I needed to go to Brazil for reasons still undetermined. When I asked for more details, I was told I should go in three months, in October 2015.

When I returned to the city, I realised I had received a message from a woman I didn't know called Marie, who had seen on social media that I was in Mongolia. Marie, also a shaman, mentioned she had been in Mongolia two years prior and felt called to contact me.

"Two years ago, while on a barren field in Mongolia, I found a set of stones that stood out. As I picked them up, I received clear instructions to take these stones on a mission to Brazil. I feel you need to be involved somehow. I am going in October." My jaw dropped. I could hardly believe the synchronicity.

A few months later, Marie, Sylvain, and I met in Brazil for the series of missions I shared at the beginning of this book.

The journey was wild, filled with ecstatic moments that felt otherworldly. To this day, I still don't fully understand what we did or its purpose apart from the fact that it was about enabling a connection to another realm, perhaps the divine, Source, or the quantum.

Sylvain was the shaman who, on our final day together in Brazil, suggested I contact Kenneth Ray Stubbs after hearing, with clarity, that I was to be a sex shaman.

## Life post-Brazil

When I returned to Barcelona, everything felt different. It became common for me to experience random waves of orgasmic pleasure overtaking me in day-to-day moments. I would get lost in the verse of a poem or staring into a cup of coffee. I would feel a passing bird's cry or a speeding motorcycle's roar as an electric wave of pleasure rippling through my body.

I settled on renting an inexpensive room in a friend's flat and lived only with a small collection of belongings on a single clothes rack and a narrow shelf. I was settling into a basic life with minimal living costs that would allow me the space to continue to "just wait" and listen to my inner voice.

For the first two months, I barely left my room. The only thing that got me out was food and water; I didn't need anything more. I was thirty-five but felt complete, like I'd retired. I felt inspired by the stories of ancient civilisations that believed humans could bring healing and impact simply by the power of their presence. I knew all I had to do was "be."

But this was contrary to Western culture, which taught me that if I were to impact the world, I must work hard, and the path would be challenging and effortful. "Nothing valuable comes easily," I had learned.

These cultural beliefs felt far away from the flow of the universal system I was now being led by: A system that involves the spinning of the earth, the rising of the moon, the movement of the tornadoes and shooting stars.

Decades of thick patterns based on doing, planning, organising and strategising had met their medicine. I realised that simply being, listening and waiting was much more powerful than "doing" anything. In the same way that I was moved effortlessly from Barcelona to Ulanbataar or invited to trek up and down mountains in Brazil, I knew that if something needed to be done by me, it would be done.

It felt right to me that, like other beings in nature, like a flower, a fruit, or even the venom of a snake, we humans should also be able to yield impact effortlessly, simply with the power of our very presence. It also felt right that this ability would awaken as I explored the connection to Source, the universal force behind the creation of all life in nature.

## Discovering shamanism

My time being mentored by Stubbs gave me a container to take this exploration further. After all, Stubbs was the first person I would see embodying this type of powerful presence. A mere 30-second video call to fix a time for the following day left me feeling something I could only describe as oneness.

It was also very fitting that Ray was known as the Sexual Shaman and had been pioneering tantra practices in the West since the 1970s. Since first hearing the words sex shaman in Brazil, I had researched and explored the various trainings that could support me on this journey. I had signed up for a sexological bodywork training that was later cancelled, an ISTA training I later decided to step out of. I had considered Body Electric and the various courses by Mantak Chia. All these trainings promised a clear result: they were facilitator trainings allowing us to learn how to share a specific practice with clients.

Instead of promising specific results, Stubbs offered a process that was quite abstract. There was no clear intention other than connecting to Source, which allowed us to develop and grow. I was introduced to a whole new facet of Tantra, which was more energetic and primordial and felt radical.

Ray's alternative, more energetic, views of Tantra had emerged following an accident that left him with quadriplegia. He decided to connect to energy because he couldn't continue facilitating the usual, more somatic tantra massage workshops.

With Ray, I explored a new, expanded definition of sex

beyond our views of penetration or mutual genital touch that often leads to ejaculation. Sex is a merging of energies, a joining of essences that allows healing and growth to take place.

I spent years being mentored by him, and most of the teaching happened via transmission, simply by sitting together and sharing energy.

We eventually co-created the Earth Energy project, which led me to connect with sacred sites around the world and catapulted this development into a different realm. I learned about energy, transmission and the connection between the realm of form and the formless.

The ceremonies had a profound impact on me. I would often find myself experiencing oneness in a way similar to my experience in Mykonos. At times, the experiences awoke sounds and movements that reminded me of my experience in Bangkok. Other times, I was forced to sit with the darkness of pain and shadows.

When faced with challenges, darkness and disruptions, I merged with them and noticed powerful resources awakening as a response. From such a continuous connection to Source, I began to experience my body as a force of nature, an ecosystem of its own.

## The gift of catastrophes in nature

When catastrophes strike in nature, the earth knows how to naturally and effortlessly awaken the resources to regulate them. For example, a forest fire creates ashes that fertilise the land's soil. Seeds are even released from the burning tree trunks, allowing a new species of trees to grow. A disastrous landslide or receding glaciers might, while catastrophic, also cause biodiversity to increase on the land. Indeed, in nature, catastrophes will often lead an ecosystem to become even more resilient than it would have been had they not taken place.

As I became attuned to this universal force, my being began to behave this way. Any challenge that arose for me was like a storm, and its damage allowed it to awaken new resources and become even more resilient.

The world around me changed during this time, and so did I. The possessive, insecure interior designer I had been pre-Mykonos became a self-assured and confident sexual shaman.

This impacted the ways I related to family members, lovers and friends. Walls came down, and creativity emerged in the form of ideas for new projects and the ability to devise solutions to challenges.

This powerful time also came with doubt and fear. Letting go of the protective structures that previously organised me led me into a mysterious and unknown realm. As strong as this medicine was, it also felt disorganised and chaotic, and I often had no idea what to do with it.

With time, I started feeling I was meant to share this process with others as a facilitator and guide, but I was still determining how.

I had trained in somatic movement therapy, but that wasn't

the most powerful part; it was a preparation and entry point. Neo-tantra didn't interest me, mainly because I didn't enjoy traditional tantric massage techniques. My primary training had been with Ray Stubbs, and he clearly didn't want any of his students to teach in the same way he did.

Training with him was meant to hold space for the emergence of our own work and gifts, whatever they were. These should be expressed and shared in a way that deeply resonates with us.

I knew full well I could only teach what I was already embodying. Since my time in Bangkok with Ray and travelling the world, I had gotten used to lying in an open space, connecting to Source and waiting to be informed by the movements and sounds that would arise through me.

## The teachings came

With this in mind, I organised my first workshop in London on the 2016 autumn equinox. Thirty-five people showed up, and I had no clue what I would teach or offer. I simply labelled it an Equinox Shamanic Ceremony (words I would not use today).

We sat together, and I gave a short lecture on whatever insights had appeared for me that day. I spoke about fear and oneness and how they were related.

I opened a sharing space in which a few people spoke from the heart, sharing a challenge or inquiry that wanted to be spoken. I replied with whatever insights came up as a response. When we ran out of words, I turned down the lights, lit candles, and invited everyone to lie down and close their eyes.

The participants were invited to do nothing—to lie down and wait. I intended to be energetically one with them and with all of existence.

But it wouldn't be long before movements and sounds emerged spontaneously and took over. I twisted, writhed, chanted, and dissolved into a realm beyond time and space until I landed into stillness, and the process was done.

Soon enough, I would notice twitches, pulses, waves, and other involuntary movements rippling across the bodies in the room. While it felt similar to what emerged in Bangkok or many places I visited, it was different. I was more lucid and could tell I was clearly holding space for the group. The process was not only mine but mostly theirs. I was transmitting. Rather than being an intimate love-making experience between me and Source, this was more of a cosmic "orgy" (energetic and clothed, of course) that involved others.

I later understood that the participants and I had become one during that practice. In that merged space, my body was perceiving their bodies' pains, challenges and disruptions, similar to how I had perceived my own over the previous years.

The spontaneous movements and sounds that arose for me were signs of the medicine that awoke within. Since we merged and mirrored each other, it awoke within them, too. This was transmission.

The responses were different for each person. Mine were possibly the strongest in the room; some were similar to mine, and some people stayed perfectly still. There was no right or wrong; it was simply about showing up and being present. Part of me thought I was crazy for simply instructing people to lie down and wait while I merged with them. I also believed that those who attended, especially those who would come back repeatedly, were even crazier. Even as movements and sounds would arise spontaneously for the participants, and it was obvious something was going on, I still doubted the process, especially since I hosted my workshops alongside other facilitators who guided people through practices that felt much less far-fetched.

As I repeated the process and people kept showing up and telling me of the impact they experienced, I began to trust it.

I taught these workshops repeatedly for approximately three years, and they evolved with time. Some people would come for one session and never return, and some would return repeatedly. If people were drawn to it, it wasn't something they could understand, but their bodies felt they needed to be there. The more committed people were, the more impact they would experience.

Some people found themselves ready and able to be more creative and fearless and even shift careers. I saw some people overcome pain from abuse they had experienced decades before, be supported in releasing drug and alcohol addictions, and let go of antidepressants.

I decided to "organise" myself and call myself a shaman and a facilitator. Some of the main teachings happened when I demonstrated how my body responds in connection to Source.

I would lie on a mat in the centre of the room and invite people to watch me with their bodies rather than their eyes and minds. I connected to Source and whatever I perceived as happening in the group and let my body move. It would writhe, twist and unravel in ways that are uncommon to most people.

In those moments, I am not showing people how to move but how I am being moved. It is all about transmission. My energy body and my fluid system communicate with those of the participants in the room. Whether they realise it or not, they are receiving information in a primordial way, which their body can choose to use and express through movement, sounds or other somatic expressions too.

I often start my workshops or sessions by telling clients that if all they did was be present for whatever time we were together, whether one hour or one week, they would have done 90% of what they've come here to do.

Some people even tune out my voice. Participants in my online workshops have even admitted to turning off the volume at times; they perceive that hearing me speak can, at times, distract them and prevent them from feeling the full transmission.

So today, when I offer shamanic ceremonies as part of a larger full-week retreat or course, I sit in focused awareness and intention with the group and invite them to feel what is in their body.

Some people shake, move, writhe and make sounds. Some will even start retching, experiencing physiological responses they say are similar to those they experienced with ayahuasca.

Other people stay still and notice very little. Others will even be triggered by the responses of others that feel violent to them or that they often identify as similar to an exorcism or being possessed by an entity.

I can remember one significant experience at a retreat in Costa Rica. Halfway through the week, several participants reported feeling sick, complaining about low energy levels, fever, and even cough and flu symptoms.

That evening, I decided to hold a simple shamanic energy ceremony. All I did was sit and merge with the 16 people, including those who indicated feeling unwell. The room was filled with varying responses. Some wailed, some cried, some moved and made sounds, some stayed still, and one even left the room, saying it was all "too much."

Interestingly, the next morning, everyone who had previously reported feeling sick felt perfectly fine, except for one person who had to leave because of serious pain in the pancreas, which indicated a more serious condition.

So what happened that night in that ceremony?

It may have been a coincidence, but the shift felt quite striking. I believe people experienced the awakening of internal resources that could support their healing. As the retreat was heavily focused on the sexual shadow, it was very likely that the illness symptoms they experienced were psycho-somatic. These symptoms of tiredness, fever, low energy, etc., may have arisen due to us making space for parts of our darker underworld to emerge and be seen.

I want to reiterate that the work of a shaman is not to try to play God or to be a healer. Our role is to transmit: to be present and bring intentionality, focus and power to any situation. To merge with it as one and share our resources with it. Energy merging is done without intention; we don't intend to heal anyone but rather share our resources, and if these can be used, they will.

**The transmission of presence**

In 2018, I started teaching a nine-month programme and was surprised to see that many students who showed up for the course shared that their intention was to get closer to developing what they called "Christ consciousness." As we discussed it more, it became clear that they were seeking to live life more closely to what they could see in Jesus Christ or Mary Magdalene, i.e., the ability to live in the world with more knowingness and bring impact by transmission and presence.

I was fascinated that so many people were voicing this desire even though I had not written about it on my website or any other promotional materials. Even writing this now, in this book, is conflicting. Our collective culture tends to shut down anything that gets close to appearing like a "God complex." I have also questioned whether this work can support the type of development these students sought.

But from a conceptual point of view, it made sense. If, after all, Jesus Christ was sent here to show us who we could be in the world, it must be possible for us to experience this development.

## Individual work with clients

Over the years of doing this work, this work has been varied. It has  held space for exorcisms, helped people release addictions, the use of antidepressants, or tenacious emotional patterns, etc.

If a person comes to me with a physical complaint, such as recurring heart pain, by simply intending to be one with them energetically, they gain access to the same abilities I have access to for the time that we are together.

In most individual client sessions, we sit together, set intentions for our explorations, and wait. At times, questions emerge, and emotional processing is required. Other times, the mind is too busy, and somatic practices are necessary to drop into a deeper state. But the highest expression of this work lies in transmission.

My being can perceive their patterns, including whatever discomfort they might be experiencing, such as heart pain or an emotional block. My being can then recognise what resources are needed to merge with the pain, and these can awaken within me. As the two of us are connected, functioning as one energetic system, the resources needed by the client will awaken within them as they have within me. I'm not healing them directly but transmitting as I share abilities that can awaken within themselves, allowing them to heal.

Suppose we were to stay connected like this recurrently, the client would eventually develop these abilities permanently and be able to support their transformation in the same way whenever they wished. Eventually, they would also gain the ability to support the transformation of others. This is why most people I work with today are facilitators or training to be facilitators.

**What the hell just happened? (If anything).**

From my experience of sitting in these potent spaces, I learnt that the impact of transmission can vary from feeling nothing and doubting the whole process to moments in which the body sensations feel intense and overwhelming. Our bodies can begin to sway, spiral, tremble, pulse and undulate.

But the highest expression of this work lies in transmission, the simple act of energy merging. The purest form of sacred intimacy between me and a client happens when we simply sit and wait. Clients often begin to move spontaneously. The energy merging usually results in twitches, pulses, waves and other random, involuntary body movements. Their breath changes, and they begin to make sounds that might even escalate into spontaneous expressions similar to those I experienced several times on my journey.

Sometimes, the experience can resemble an actual physiological orgasm. Clients will throw their heads back, their spines undulate, and arch and their eyes roll back. They might grip the mat underneath them, the blankets or even my clothes. Their pelvic area might begin to tilt, thrust and rock, and energy which feels more sexual will arise. Often, male clients will get an erection, and some of them will even ejaculate without any touch or sexual contact.

All this can happen from the waves of energy arising in their bodies due to this intentional energy merging. The important part about sitting together in an open space is being aware that we're connected to something greater. The work doesn't rely on what happens in that moment but rather on all the preparation that came beforehand to allow this cosmic connection.

With time, my work became highly explicit and sexual. Clients with heavy sexual trauma showed up seeking resolution. I knew I could support them like I had supported others.

I realised that for many of these clients, enacting sexual acts would often awaken strong emotions and sensations relating to trauma, pain and shame. I became a sex shaman, a sacred prostitute.

Engaging in sexual acts with clients would open up a gateway to wounds and stories that needed to be held and loved. As these would awaken, we would sit and merge with them. Whatever suppression might have existed in their energy body could connect with the unsuppressed energies of the Source. These parts of themselves that felt dark, inadequate and wounded could find love.

At times I would tie clients up, role-play aggression, or even simulate rape, piss on them, or slap them. At times, they might come with one of these intentions, but all they needed was to be held.

**Case study: Jerome the sex-offender**

One of my most meaningful client sessions happened with a man called Jerome in Paris. He was a sex offender who had just been released on parole and was under strict supervision. He had been convicted of sexual assault on a minor who was 11 years old at the time.

"I know what I did was wrong. I know what I need to do to fix it, and I need help. I know you are the person who will help me." He wrote me.

When we met, I was surprised by him. He was in his early seventies, slim, with his hair parted to the side. He wore a pair of metal glasses and a plaid short-sleeved shirt, radiating softness and kindness in a way most people don't.

We sat on the bed, and he spoke more about his situation. He had been raised by a loving father. Then, at the age of 11, as he approached puberty, his father disconnected from him. The hugs stopped and were replaced by demands for him to toughen up and "be a man".

He realised that by connecting with an 11-year-old boy, he was seeking to repair the disconnection that had happened to him at that age. Interestingly, when I told him I was 42 at the time of the session, he mentioned his father was the same age when he was 11, and the disconnection occurred.

Although I don't approve of it and in no way support anyone engaging in any sexual interaction that would be illegal or immoral, part of my job is to find a neutral space of love, compassion and understanding for it. Especially when one approaches it the way that Jerome did.

Jerome had mentioned in his email that he knew what he needed, and I asked him what that was. He needed to be held like his father had held him before the disconnection. That was all.

I lay in bed holding this 72-year-old man, and I was his father. As we lay together, we were transported to a time 61 years prior when the disconnection occurred. Together, we held that space with love and safety.

He sighed, melted into me and started to cry. We lay there for the rest of the session, him sobbing and me simply holding him.

The 11-year-old self simply needed love. Although we cuddled and words were spoken, it was clear that something more significant had occurred.

Through our energy merging, his 11-year-old wounded and hurt little boy had access to new resources that could hopefully support him as he faced adversity.

Even as my work became sexual and explicit, and clients often expect intense sexual experiences, the most powerful part of the work lies not in the touch or interaction but in what happens in the unseen.

We sit together, merge and transmit. This was the most powerful and truthful version of this work.

**I learned love**

I wrote earlier that my being began to behave like its own ecosystem, in which catastrophes often enabled new resources to awaken. The most important resource that arose for me was love.

There were many moments on this journey when I experienced fear, anxiety and even terror. I was leaving behind cultural systems that I believed had kept me safe. I was invited to trust the unseen, a force that couldn't be touched, measured or proven.

I had to let go of lovers, friends, and traditional jobs that felt safe. Fear manifested as waves of uncomfortable and overwhelming sensations. My first impulse was to fight or escape them, but I knew I had to merge with them.

As I became one with them and let the process run its course, new sensations arose and flooded my being as a response. These were expressions of the force of love.

Beyond simply saying the words "I love you" or "I love me", beyond wanting the best for someone or wanting them in my life, I learned that love was an embodied medicine.

I learned that love is a force of nature that exists within me. "True love" can not be understood by the mind but rather felt in the body. It's an elemental, energetic and somatic force that can't be described in words because words would limit it.

I learned that love is an expression of the creation of life that exists in the body and emerges from Source. Like creation in nature comes from chaos, love, for me, had arisen as a medicine for fear and darkness.

Experiencing challenges in my body taught me about love, mainly that love is oneness.

**Love is oneness**

If fear leads us to protect ourselves and separate and divide ourselves from others, the medicine to this division is oneness. As love is the medicine for fear, love would also be oneness. Love is a life force, the very fabric of the universe.

When connected to Source, my being vibrates, i.e., functions more primordially than usual. This primordial state (which relates to the cosmic anatomy) is beyond the typical limitations that bind me to the limited self that might be organised by fear and trying to protect itself.

The longer I spend in that state, the less I am entrained in patterns of limitations and fears and the more I am entrained in patterns of Source and love. This state is primordial, pre-verbal, pre-trauma, and pre-conditioning. Spending extended time in this primordial "pre-space" connecting to Source allowed a radical shift.

Although love is a response to fear, it is not its opposite, nor is it the opposite of hate. As oneness, love is non-dual; love is neutral. Understanding love as neutral made it easier for me, as an energy being, a sex shaman, and a sacred prostitute, to love every part of myself but also help others bring love to every aspect of themselves.

When I sit with a client who is a convicted paedophile, a rapist, a sex offender, etc., I can offer that part of them love, not by saying "I love you" nor by saying it's right or wrong. I offer that part of them love by merging with it, offering it oneness and neutrality.

Merging with something, i.e. being in oneness with it, is the best way to show it love. In oneness, I release all defense from it. I intend to vibrate like it, acknowledging it as a part of me, too. As I merge with it, I offer it the highest resources available within me to become available to it, too.

In chapter 6, we saw that neutrality exists in our sensations, which are the first order of perception.

As an embodied medicine, love also exists in sensations, such as the flood of subtle tingles and pulsations that arose within me as I sat with fear and terror.

So when I sit and merge with someone, I perceive whatever is happening within them as sensations in my body. For instance, my body can perceive sensations relating to a heart problem, an emotional issue, an addiction, or other concerning behaviours like, for example, paedophilia. I can merge with those sensations and meet them with the embodied medicine of love. The two can meet, and healing can take place.

While it might sound crazy to say that I would want to merge with the energy or frequencies behind something like sexual abuse, paedophilia, etc., this is part of the journey to oneness. Oneness is not exclusive; it must include everything.

When I merge with these energies, I recognise that, at their root, they are merely neutral frequencies that are also part of the great oneness of everything.
Any distortion, such as paedophilia, abuse etc., is simply the result of a protective mechanism resulting from experiencing circumstances one was incapable to hold at the time.

My job, as a sex shaman, sacred prostitute, and energy being, is to offer these distortions resources. Whether these heal or return to balance is not up to me. I have no control over that, nor do I want any. My job is to share and offer resources and love which become available to the other.

# 9B

# THE ACCIDENT: A SPECIAL ADDENDUM TO CHAPTER 10

*The following pages were not originally planned to be part of this book, but following a serendipitous sequence of events, I felt they needed to be shared.*

In Chapter 9, I discussed how the ongoing practice of energy merging taught me to experience life like a natural ecosystem. Just as nature responds to catastrophic events, I discovered that I too could awaken and tap into new resources when faced with grave challenges. Most importantly, this process would enable me to emerge stronger after a catastrophe than I would have been had the event never happened.

**The accident**

As I typed the last key of the chapter and closed my laptop, the universe provided me with a circumstance that would allow me to experience this in real time.

It was a warm and sunny morning on Tuesday, August 06 2024, at 8:45 am. I had just completed chapter 9, the final one of the body of this manuscript and decided to get on with other tasks before returning to write the conclusion later.

For the last three days, my bicycle brakes had begun to malfunction. The bike shop had been closed for a couple of days but reopened that Tuesday morning, so I decided to head down to get them fixed after completing the chapter.

I headed down as usual, exiting the house garage with my electric bike, aware I needed to be careful as I would be cycling down a steep hill.

As I cycled down carefully, I noticed the breaks were worse than I thought. Breaking as hard as I could allowed the bike to slow down but not stop. It was a heavy electric bike, so I knew placing my foot on the ground to stop it could injure my leg.

I headed down a very sharp left turn down a hill that would soon get steeper. As I freewheeled, unable to stop my bike, I needed to make a snap decision that could potentially change my life.

I had two options. The first was to continue straight and freewheel into a busy roundabout, which, if I survived, would lead me to a second, busier roundabout that led to a busy highway. The second option was to turn right towards a brick wall.

In the blink of an eye, I chose the wall.

Had I chosen the roundabout, the passing cars would have likely swerved to miss me and perhaps cursed at me, unaware of my predicament. But I decided not to chance it and preferred to keep my fate in my own hands.

I aimed for the wall, hoping to use my leg to break the fall and make it as painless as possible.

I blacked out. When I came back to consciousness, I found myself faced with a kind man assuring me everything would be okay. An ambulance was on its way, everything would be fine. I noticed I was covered in blood but did not understand the severity of what I had experienced until the ambulance arrived.

They thanked the man for his help, laid me on a stretcher and showed me my face with a mirror. A giant hole resembling a crevice of the moon had torn across my forehead near my eyebrow, gushing with blood as flesh dangled out. An even larger hole had torn across my right knee, and my feet, shoulders and wrists were bleeding too. Still, as the man had said, I knew I would be fine.

I spent the following hours at the hospital being stitched up, MRI-scanned, bandaged, etc. The whole time, the irony of the situation was not lost on me. I had literally just closed my laptop after writing about learning to operate like an ecosystem in nature when faced with catastrophe, and here I was at the hospital in critical condition. I knew exactly what was going on.

I knew the universe had sent me a circumstance that would allow me to trust the teachings even more and I snickered as I reflected on it. Indeed, everything was exactly as it should be.

Sure, I was uncomfortable. My entire body ached like hell. I was banged up and needed to cancel upcoming work plans, which would lead to a loss of revenue. But I knew everything was exactly as it should be.

## The backstory

In the weeks before this incident, I had been experiencing a strong intuitive sense that a big change was coming my way. Not a change of career, a move to a new city, or a new life partner, but rather a change in the way I would be in the world.

My father, who had been very ill for the last two years, had just entered the final stages of his life and was beginning to transition out of physical form. For the two years of his illness, the world felt different. I probably looked and felt the same to those around me, but inside, I felt less settled and safe. As I sat with it, I realised that although I was quite independent, even living thousands of kilometres away from my family, an unconscious part of me was still tethering to my parents, especially my father, for safety. In the past few weeks, as he was entering palliative care, the feeling was intensifying.

On the surface, I knew life was fine and I was safe. But an unconscious programme operating in the shadows destabilised me.

I found myself clinging to certain attachments in ways that were uncharacteristic for me. I even used sex, digital media and my work as a way of escaping. I knew I could do better.

Intuitively, I kept seeing images of the archetypes of these super-power beings I have written about throughout this book, such as the Dalai Lama, certain rinpoches, and others. I knew that the resources that were available to them were available to me, too. I knew I could walk through the world more "easefully" than I was. The destination was clear, but the journey wasn't. I was stuck, unable to get clarity on how the shift would take place.

As I lay on the hospital bed, in pain, surrounded by a team of specialists, I realised the process that would lead to this shift was under way.

This accident would allow me to trust more, and the sense of unease and anxiety would find its medicine. I needed to believe, more than I already did, that even if catastrophe struck, I would be held, supported, acknowledged, and loved.

So, under the pretext of faulty bike breaks, I "threw myself" at a wall to prove that I was right. I could indeed trust.

In the blink of an eye, a guardian angel, a skilled ambulance team, and a team of medical specialists gathered around me. Friends called and came to visit, even taking me home to care for me. It was clear: I was cared for, acknowledged, and loved.

More importantly, my relationships to some of my main attachments was tested. I would have to cancel work plans, resulting in lost income and uncertainty. Stitches and bruises across my face and body and pains on my wrists, knees, and feet would keep me from my usual favourite activities.

Using sex, digital media or even work to bypass became uncomfortable, even impossible. I could do nothing else but pause, slow down, and give myself space to truly maintain the connection to Source as deeply and consistently as I knew I could. This experience helped me build a new foundational baseline of resources that would be accessible to me continuously.

The accident had come like a tsunami, which, while disastrous at first, could also magically reshape a coastline, create new habitats for endangered species and help renew a declining ecosystem.

The work was done. The accident that had rocked my body also shattered the layer of unease that had surrounded it. My trust in the universe deepened, and my connection to the non-local forces- and to love- became stronger.

# CONCLUSION

So now you have reached the end of this book and I hope you have enjoyed reading it as much as I have enjoyed birthing it.

I hope it will carry on the legacy of teachers, shamans, and civilisations of the past in a way that is useful for the "here and now."

I hope it has helped clarify your understanding of oneness and energy merging, both as an intrinsic function of our being and as an intentional healing practice you will hopefully feel called to embrace.

I also hope it has helped deepen your understanding of the world of the unseen, and that it has shown you that you are more than you think; that beyond the limited perceptions of ourselves and of existence, there is much more available.

I hope it has demonstrated that each of us can indeed have access to the entirety of the universe at any moment, should we choose to allow it.

I hope this book has taught you the power and possibility that can be accessed through an intentional practice of achieving oneness.

## In summary

I started this book by sharing about my shamanic missions in Brazil, during which we supported the development of an access point to Source. Our work was inspired by ancient civilisations who believed humans could bring impact to others simply by the power of their presence.

When we develop this power, we become energy beings, able to impact others through the power of transmission. In order to transmit, the energy being must have the ability to achieve oneness and energy merging.

Science shows us that we are all made of interpenetrating frequency waves. Because of this, we are all able to be in oneness and merge energetically. Energy merging is, therefore, a function that is intrinsic to all humans. However, it requires us to develop and awaken dormant abilities. Without these abilities, we can only achieve oneness while in Orgasm.

Some humans like the Dalai Lama, a child who may have been chosen to be the rinpoche of a monastery at the age of 3, might be born with these abilities, but we can all awaken them.

This development and awakening comes from an intentional process of energy merging by which we connect continuously with Source.

We begin by establishing a connection to Source within us.

We then stay in this connection for a continuous period.

After sustaining this connection long enough, we become developed enough to transmit and share this energy with others.

As well as being a process of energetic development, it is also a process of lovemaking with every part of the self. We look at our shadows and pains but also our greatest gifts and power.

In this process, we develop the ability to vibrate like more of existence.

Eventually, we can vibrate like all of existence, i.e. the 5 planes that make up our universe. Each plane is a different level of energetic density that exists within us. When we can vibrate like all of existence, we can achieve oneness through an intentional process. We are able to merge with (and vibrate like) more energetic systems; trees, stones, or other human beings.

As facilitators, sacred intimates, sex shamans, sacred prostitutes, we have the ability to connect with others and hold space for their transformation through this merging.

As we merge energetically, we vibrate like each other and the abilities available to us become available to them, too. Eventually, the more time we stay in the connection, the more the abilities become permanent for them and they can facilitate others as well.

I also shared my journey with this work, from the break-up in Mykonos that led to my first oneness experience, to the series of circumstances that led me to Brazil on my first shamanic missions. Following these missions, I met Kenneth Ray Stubbs, the first example of a living energy being I had ever encountered.

Working with him held space for my understanding of shamanism and the development of the work I am here to do. Today, this includes my work as a sex shaman and sacred prostitute, holding space for the healing of others through sexuality.

Most importantly, through this process, I learned love. Not simply the love that refers to being "in love" or wanting the best for someone, but rather love as an embodied medicine beyond words. This love came from being in continuous connection to Source and entraining to the flow of life, the force behind all creation. It appeared as a wave of sensations and frequencies that arose in my body as a response to fear and anxiety. As I merged with fear, love arose.

When attuned to this force, I behave like a natural ecosystem. If catastrophes occur, resources will automatically awaken in response, leaving me in a better state than I would have been if the disaster had not happened at all.

This leads me to the knowingness that everything, no matter how challenging it might appear, is exactly as it should be.

## A new vocation?

Perhaps reading this book has also awakened a new calling for you: to engage on a new path of growth and development and facilitate others.

Perhaps you feel called to be an energy being, a shaman, or even a sacred prostitute.

## How do I know if I am an energy being?

Traditionally, a shaman would be told by an elder or other peers that they are now a shaman too. At 3, a child might be taken from their family and told they were meant to be the next rinpoche of a monastery.

As we move into times less organised by lineage, this sort of initiation or rites of passage could happen differently, in less traditional ways.

We all have access to tools for our growth and development, which might include the support of a teacher, a sacred site, or our own inner guidance.

After continuous practice, one might receive a clear call to serve others. In that case, one might reach out to an elder or another shaman and ask for their point of view.

In my case, I was led on a path that seemed drawn for me. It started when I was told I was a shaman and invited to Mongolia within 24 hours. It continued in Bangkok during a 13-hour experience of spontaneous connection to Source and in Brazil on the shamanic missions with Marie and Sylvain.

But the real call happened on my own, when I entered into dialogue with Source and saw images of what would come next. I saw visions of workshops and participants and received direct and clear insights about the materials I would teach. I saw how the mission of being a sex shaman would finally come into form years after first hearing those words in Brazil.

Students and aspiring facilitators often ask me to tell them if I think they are a shaman or not. I generally answer with the following question:

"What call do you feel within you?
What do you hear when you listen to your body?
What is meant to be done by you in the world?"

Whether or not we were told we are an energy being or a shaman, traditionally, if a vocation is meant to call us, it will. If work is meant to be done by us, it will.

The universe will conspire to enable it.

This doesn't mean that we should be passive or disengaged. We must create a potent space to listen and dialogue with Source. This process and this book are all about creating this space.

We must cultivate a direct connection with our body to hear the source of life pulsating within, speaking to us, through us and for us.

We must actively seek silence and stillness to truly hear this voice speak.

We must live differently from those around us, turning away from distractions, indulgences and attachments, to create spaces where introspection can occur and inspiration and innovation can take place.

We must also be ok with the boredom, and even FOMO (fear of missing out) which may result from it.

In my case, I found it useful to rent an inexpensive room in a friend's flat while I was going through this process. Not worrying about money allowed me to wait and follow the instruction to "do nothing." It allowed me to listen and trust the process more deeply. Most importantly, it allowed me to remain free of any agenda, unattached to any outcome. I gave myself the space to listen to my body and the Source of life vibrating through it.

The process will be different for each of us.

## A way of life

Beyond being a facilitator, a shaman, a sacred prostitute or other, being an energy being is a vocation, a way of life. It is not something we switch on or off or punch in and out of on a timer.

It is who we are every day, in every moment.

The "super beings" I have written about across this book, such as Jesus Christ, the Dalai Lama, the rinpoche chosen at the age of 3, Amma the hugging saint, or the sages mentioned by Joseph Selbie, are all archetypal expressions of this full-time energy being. They move through the world with the unfolding of life and impart healing simply with the power of their presence.

But while this may be a vocation that calls just a few of us, it is available to all.

According to Kenneth Ray Stubbs, the Dalai Lama, a few rinpoches and even some of us who were his closer students have developed a fully functioning rainbow body. In chapter 4, we saw that the rainbow body is our 21st energetic structure; it can only be developed when the 20 others have been fully developed. Having a fully functioning rainbow body means one can access all the energy of Source at all times, should we choose to turn towards it.

## Life as an energy being

So what does life as an energy being look and feel like?
How would we live if we knew we could always access the
energy of Source?

*

As energy beings,
We are "in the world but not of it."

We fully engage in the "cultural context" while maintaining a
direct and continuous connection to Source.

In every moment, we know we can choose to turn towards
the medicine that is already, and always, here for us.

Life becomes a "living prayer" in which every moment,
occurrence, being, character, and object is sacred.

We can choose to merge energetically at any moment, at any
time.

As we merge with the source, we can remember that the
power of all existence is available to us at any moment.
We live in direct engagement with the universal force that
pulsates and vibrates through us, for us.

We can choose to merge with parts of ourselves when we
feel they need love, care, and awareness to come back to
alignment. Life becomes a continuous process of development
and personal growth.

We can merge with whatever we face, whether nourishing or challenging, and intend to be fully one with it.

We can merge with anything outside us, any person, being, animal, or circumstance, and share our resources with them too.

We can experience anything external to us, whether painful or pleasurable, as waves of soft vibrations rippling through our cells.

We are fully present with every moment, knowing we are also connected to something greater than it.

We can feel the deepest pains and greatest pleasures while feeling the power of the formless within us, reminding us all is well. We can laugh, cry, kiss and fall in love, all while marching to the beat of the cosmic drum.

We can thrive in the face of adversity, able to see the gift in everything, in every moment.

We see our body as an ecosystem experiencing every catastrophe or crisis as an initiation, rite of passage, and opportunity for growth.

Everything, as it is, is exactly as it should be.

Ordinary occurrences, like drinking a coffee or going to the ATM, could become orgasmic and "other-worldly."

In experiencing this power for ourselves, we can share it with others too.

We become medicine holders, innovators, and transmitters, supporting the healing of others with little or no words or actions.

*

But this doesn't mean that life is perfect.
Indeed, it can sometimes suck.

The flow will challenge us,
swallow us up,
and spit us out.

We are, after all, here to have a human experience that will inevitably be imperfect.

The energy being is not meant to experience life as perfect in every moment, nor are we meant to be perfect in every moment.

We merge with imperfection, too.

We commit to doing our best, to be intentional and present, and to be one with every moment.

From the outside, our lives might not appear different from anyone else's, but in every moment, we know we are held, we are loved, and we are love.